# Never Give Up

*A Memoir of Resilience, Purpose, and Becoming the Change*

**Gary Jenkins, D.A., MPA,**

Former Commissioner, Department of Social Services

SWEET Institute Publishing

Transformational Books for a Transformational World

**Published by:**

SWEET Institute Publishing

New York, NY

WWW.SWEETInstitutePublishing.com

First Edition

Printed in the United States of America

ISBN (Paperback): 978-1-968105-18-1

Cover Design by SWEET Institute Publishing

Interior Design and Layout by SWEET Institute Publishing

Photo by Francisco (Frank) Gutierrez

For bulk orders, permissions, or media inquiries, please contact:

sweetinstitutepublishing@sweetinstitute.com

Unless otherwise noted, all stories and case examples in this book are either fictionalized or used with permission, and identifying details have been changed to protect the privacy of individuals.

SWEET Institute Publishing
Transformational Books for a Transformational World

**SWEET Institute Publishing**

**Universal Disclaimer**

The content provided is for educational and reflective purposes only. It is not intended to diagnose, treat, or replace professional medical or psychological care. Readers are encouraged to seek professional help when needed.

By engaging with SWEET Institute Publishing materials, you acknowledge that the authors, editors, and publishers are providing information and education, not medical or psychological services, and assume no liability for any actions or outcomes based on the information provided.

# Dedication

To my wife,
Randa Henry Jenkins,
whose love, wisdom, and unwavering support have been the bedrock
of my journey.

And to our three beautiful daughters,
Lauren, Morgan, and Jordan,
whose brilliance, strength, and light continue to inspire me every
single day.

You are my heart.
You are my why.
This is for you.

**Other Titles from SWEET Institute Publishing**

- 50 SWEET Poems: Reflections on Life, Love, and Self
- Always Enough: The Transformational Power of Unconditional Positive Regard: How to See, Accept, and Elevate Yourself and Others Through the 4 Layers of Transformation
- Because of Us: Why Outcomes Change When We Do
- Becoming the Very Best
- Before Anything Else, Validate: The Missing Link in Healing, Leadership, Relationships, and Personal Growth
- Determined to See: A Science-Based and Story-Driven Integration of A Course in Miracles and the Four Layers of Transformation
- Discovering Your Worth: Everything You Need to Feel Fulfilled
- Emotional Intelligence: The Inner Science of Transformation
- It's All Perfect: What If Nothing in Your Life Was a Mistake?
- Journey to Empowerment
- Life Is Not Hard: A New Blueprint for Living with Ease, Meaning, and Freedom
- NLP for Clinicians
- One Habit at a Time: The Art and Science of Sustainable Change
- Remembering: The Journey Back to the Pre-Conditioned Self
- Rewriting the Script: The Power of Transforming Inner Dialogue in Oppressed Communities
- The Anxiety Course: The Workbook
- The Clinician's Mirror: A Story of Projection, Self-Awareness, and Transformation for Clinicians
- The Courage to Care: Stories of Healing, Hope, and the Power of Social Work — Told by Over 50 SWEET Institute Social Workers
- The Power of Belief: How Ideas Shape Leaders, Nations, and the Future
- The Power of Faith: A Harvard-Trained Psychiatrist Speaking on Faith

- The Psychotherapy Certificate Course: The Clinician and Coach Manual (Books 1–3)
- The Secret Is in Remembering: Why We Suffer, Why We Forget, and How to Return to Who We Are
- Transforming Team Relationships from the Inside Out: The SWEET Healing Circle for Agencies — Redefining Accountability, Collaboration, and Culture
- What's Missing
- Unshakable Women: Reclaiming Power, Purpose, and Presence in Leadership

# Praise for Never Give Up

"A courageous, purpose-driven man who has never lost his humanity. This memoir is a blueprint for authentic leadership rooted in love and legacy. Read it, rise, and never give up."

**Honorable Edolphus Towns**
Former U.S. Congressman, Chair of House Committee on Oversight and Government Reform

"Gary P. Jenkins reminds us that grace and grit can coexist. This book is a masterclass in perseverance and personal transformation

**Rev. A. R. Bernard**
Founder & CEO, Christian Cultural Center

A brilliant work of truth and testimony. Chairman Jenkins speaks for a generation of Black men who were taught to be silent about their pain. This book changes that.

**Dr. Charles J. Gibbs, Ed.D.**
President, Metropolitan College of New York

"Gary P. Jenkins is the kind of leader whose story shifts paradigms. Never Give Up is more than a memoir. It's a call to rise, to lead with integrity, and to build with heart. His transparency, strength, and deep love for people make this book a legacy in motion. I am honored to know him and even more honored to learn from his journey."

**— Lu-Shawn M. Thompson**

Entrepreneur & Real Estate Investor

"Heartfelt, inspiring, and necessary. A memoir that reaches into the soul of every reader who has ever felt unseen and shows them the way back to themselves."

**Rev. Dr. Kevin D. Miller**

From humble beginnings to historic heights, Gary P. Jenkins proves that you don't need permission to become extraordinary. Read this if you need to believe again.

**Schamiqua Young D'Amato**
Assistant Deputy Commissioner, City of New York

"Few people have the ability to navigate systems and hearts at the same time. Gary P. Jenkins is that rare leader. His story belongs in boardrooms, classrooms, shelters, and homes across this nation."

**Greville French, LMSW**
Retired, NYC Department of Education

I've seen my Godfather Gary behind the curtain. This book captures what I've always known—he leads with love, lives with truth, and never gives up on people, including himself.

**Anthony Regester**
The Godson!

"This book should be required reading for every public servant. Gary's journey is a beacon—a reminder that public leadership must begin with personal integrity and radical empathy."

**NY State Assemblymember Brian A. Cunningham**

"Gary P. Jenkins delivers a powerful and deeply human narrative. His memoir is more than a story-it is a testament to resilience, faith, and the unbreakable spirit of community, enlightened, and forever change."

**Annette Holm Carela**
Retired, City of New York, Department of Social Services

# Table of Contents

# Foreword

**By Jennifer Jones Austin**

Lawyer, Social Policy Advocate, Author, Nonprofit CEO, and Daughter of the Movement

Gary Jenkins makes living and leading with your whole self appear easy, but it isn't. To authentically bring to any table all of yourself, shaped by experiences both good and bad, is for most a frightening undertaking. For many, such vulnerability and openness is shunned, often subconsciously.

Fortunately for us, Gary Jenkins isn't wired this way. He understands that impactful living and leading is based in truth telling, enabling us to see ourselves and each other, and to grow in grace to overcome and achieve our life goals.

For this singular reason I am excited about Jenkins' memoir, *Never Give Up.* Having endured a myriad of adverse childhood experiences but also boundless love and encouragement from those who mattered, and then building a successful career in human services caring for people made vulnerable, Jenkins knows that at all times somewhere there is a person staring into the night, believing the odds will swallow them whole. He knows a parent is grieving, a leader is breaking, and a dreamer is questioning whether their journey matters. Gary writes and shares his life's story for them. He tells his truth for all of us.

While reading *Never Give Up,* I was reminded all at once of my friend and former boss, the late Nicholas Scoppetta. In his early years Scoppetta was in foster care, and decades later in the 1990's he led child welfare reform in New York City. Scoppetta would say, "I'm not who I am despite my circumstances; rather, I am who I am because of my circumstances." I thought of my big brother, friend, and leader in the struggle, the Reverend Al Sharpton, whose adverse experiences as a child could have caused him to turn from his calling but instead served to strengthen him, resulting in him becoming the longest serving civil rights leader of all time. His life too is a reminder that *"it's not where you start but how you finish"*. And I thought of the profound words of the successful, young businessperson who I sat next to and talked with for the entire length of a six-hour flight: "Inspiring others is the most God-like thing you can do."

In just about every page of *Never give up*, I couldn't help but see them and many more individuals, and also myself. For in sharing his life story in such a vulnerable and humbling manner, Jenkins invites us to let down our guardrails and reflect on the storms we each have known and the imprints they have on our lives. It's the honesty with which he writes that draws us in. He names depression, doubt, and the ways we all wear masks to survive, even when we are succeeding. In doing so, he inspires us to see, accept and embrace the totality and impact of our truths.

Just as importantly, Jenkins emboldens us to find strength in our struggles. True to form, Jenkins writes with fluid honesty and openness, enabling us to better understand how our past informs our present and our future in real time and over time, and how our awareness and appreciation of the impact of our past changes overtime, helping us to grow and see the possibilities within us.

*Never Give Up* is powerfully resonating, in great part because it's so familiar and relatable and yet it's transcendent. Jenkins writes because he understands that truth-telling, in the tradition of our ancestors, is both a responsibility and a sacred offering. He writes because his suffering, while personal, offers up communal healing. He writes because he knows, as the great hymn "If I Can Help Somebody," written by Alma Irene Bazel Androzzo Thompson in 1945, admonishes, "If I can help somebody as I pass along, if I can cheer somebody with a word or song, if I can show somebody he is traveling wrong, then my living shall not be in vain".

There are books that inform. There are books that inspire. *Never Give Up* does these things and more, for it is a mirror for those who are searching, a map for those who are lost, and a balm for those who are wounded by the silence of their own story. It is a call to action, to embrace the power that can be sourced from struggle and vulnerability, so you can live a rewarding life and experience the joy that is your birthright.

—Jennifer Jones Austin
Lawyer, Social Policy Advocate, Author, Nonprofit CEO, and Daughter of the Movement

# Preface

**By Jocelynne Rainey, Ed.D.**

President & CEO, Brooklyn Org

We live in a world that often undervalues resilience; a world that fails to recognize the courage it takes to survive, and not just one moment of adversity, but a lifetime of it. We live in a world that measures worth by titles, resumes, and press releases, forgetting that some of the most powerful human stories will never be in to a LinkedIn profile or a news headline.

This book, Never give up: A Memoir of Resilience, Purpose, and Becoming the Change, is a necessary act of defiance against that forgetfulness. It is a living, breathing testimony to the truth that grace lives in grit, that healing is messy and sacred, and that leadership doesn't start when we arrive at the top; rather, it begins when we choose not to quit.

Gary Jenkins is a leader in every sense of the word; but not just because he served as Commissioner; and not because of the long hours he gave, the teams he built, or the systems he tried to change from within. He is a leader because he dared to keep walking even when the path was dark, even when no one was clapping, and even when he couldn't see a way out.

He is a leader because he never gave up on people, even when they had long given up on themselves.

He is a leader because he refused to let his past cancel his future.

This memoir is not a victory lap. It is not a sanitized tale of how one man climbed a ladder.

It is raw. It's unflinching. It's beautifully human.

Gary takes us back to the boy who watched his mother struggle and his sisters carry weight they shouldn't have had to. He lets us into the memories of dropped dreams, almost-failures, and doors that seemed sealed shut. He introduces us to the people who held him, challenged him, lifted him, to the mentors who became mirrors, and the colleagues who became chosen family. He then invites us into the quiet reckonings: the grief, the doubt, the heartbreak, and the long walk back to himself.

And through it all, one message echoes:

Your past is not your prison. Your pain is not your end. You were always the light.

This book will move you to tears; but also to action. It will remind you why your story matters, no matter how unfinished it feels. It will challenge every leader, advocate, social worker, policymaker, and human being who reads it to reimagine what real success looks like, and not just titles, but transformation; and not just performance, but presence.

I am honored to know Gary. I am honored to call him a peer, a brother, and a fellow warrior in this lifelong work of justice and healing. I am even more honored to introduce you to the man behind the title, behind the story, and behind the strength.

Read this book not with your eyes—but with your heart.

Let it remind you that you, too, are still becoming.

And let it dare you to tell your own truth.

Never give up.

Not now.

Not ever.

—Jocelynne Rainey, Ed.D.

President & CEO, Brooklyn Org
Brooklyn, New York

# Introduction

**By Mardoche Sidor, MD**

Medical Director, Urban Pathways
CEO, SWEET Institute
Quadruple-Board Certified Psychiatrist
Former Assistant Clinical Professor of Psychiatry, Columbia
University

There are people you meet in life who remind you what excellence looks like. There are people who make you pause and say: "Ah, this is what integrity, commitment, and soul-driven leadership look like in motion." For me, Gary is one of those people.

I have had the honor of working alongside Gary in some of the most complex, demanding, and mission-critical situations. I have witnessed him lead not just with vision, but with vulnerability, strength, and a profound love for people. What makes Gary truly rare is that he leads not to be seen, but to see others. He lifts so others can rise.

However, to truly understand this man, you must know his story. That's why this book matters.

## A Story That Needed to Be Told

Never Give Up is not just a memoir; it is a mirror for anyone who has ever questioned their worth, doubted their potential, or wondered if they could rise after life knocked them down. It is the testimony of a Black boy growing up in the shadows of loss, poverty, and low expectations, and choosing to write a different story. It is a story of persistence, a story of community, a story of faith, and a story of love.

When Gary says, "Never give up," it's not a motivational phrase; it's a battle cry from someone who has faced the edge and come back not just standing, but lifting others in the process.

## Why This Story Matters Now

We live in a time where despair can feel loud and relentless; where leaders are expected to be flawless, not human; where Black men in power still bear the burden of being seen as symbols, not souls; and where our systems often forget the people they were designed to serve.

That is why Gary's story is revolutionary, for this is a book about a man who didn't just climb the ranks, but who rebuilt the ladder. This is about a man who didn't just survive injustice, but who chose to lead with empathy; and this is about a man who didn't just serve systems, but who transformed them, from the inside out.

You'll read about the mother he lost, the mentors who believed, the dreams he whispered to himself as a young man, and the positions of power he now holds. You'll see why his relationship with his brothers in Sigma, his leadership at Metropolitan College of New York, and his vision at Urban Pathways are so remarkable; and you'll meet the man behind it all: humble, kind, brilliant, and deeply human.

## To Know Gary Is to Know Purpose

I have seen Gary in the boardroom. I have seen him at the 9th Avenue drop-in center. I have seen him with residents, staff, elected officials, and students; and in every room, he is the same: a problem solver, intelligent, funny, consistent, calm, compassionate, and committed to his work. He doesn't chase recognition. He carries responsibility.

He understands something too many leaders forget: We don't rise by titles; we rise by our integrity; and we leave legacy not through ego, but through impact.

## This Book Will Change You

As a psychiatrist, I know the neuroscience of trauma and healing. I know the layers we carry from childhood, the silent griefs, and the masks we wear. This book touches those layers; not with clinical detachment, but with deep connection. Gary doesn't just share facts; he shares feelings. He doesn't just name moments; he brings them to life.

You will cry. You will laugh. You will pause to reflect; and by the end, you will remember the places in your own story where you, too, chose not to give up.

## A Final Word

There's a reason this book begins and ends with the truth that you were never alone. Because Gary knows that healing is communal, that leadership is relational, and that legacy is not built in isolation, but in the trenches, in the neighborhoods, in the losses, in the classrooms, in the late nights and early mornings, and in the silent choices no one sees.

Gary has written a gift; a gift to young Black boys who wonder if they'll make it; a gift to mothers who sacrifice everything; and a gift to city workers, to educators, to civil servants, to anyone who has ever been underestimated.

He has written a gift to all of us who believe that resilience is real, love is power, and the climb is worth it.

Read this book slowly. Let it enter you; and then rise, again and again; and keep becoming the change.

Because as Gary shows us, you were always the light; and You are to NEVER Give UP.


—Mardoche Sidor, MD

Urban Pathways | SWEET Institute | Columbia University
New York City

# Introduction: You Were Never Alone

*A letter to the reader. Why this book exists. The truth about pain, hope, and why telling your story matters.*

**Dear Reader,**

If you've picked up this book, you might be searching for something, a way forward, a glimpse of hope, a sign that the road you're on leads somewhere. You are standing, perhaps, at a crossroads, or perhaps you've already fallen more times than you care to admit. Regardless, I wrote this for you.

This isn't a book about perfection or pretending everything's okay. It's about what it means to grow up in a world that feels like it wasn't built for you, a world where the system is stacked, the odds are long, and the voices telling you to "be realistic" are often louder than the ones telling you to dream. I'm here to tell you, **you're not alone**.

I grew up in a neighborhood filled with struggle. Drugs, poverty, incarceration, and loss weren't just things I saw on TV; rather, they were my reality. However, even amidst the chaos, there were flickers of light: a sister who believed in me, a mother who did her best, strangers who stepped in when I needed a hand, and a voice inside me that whispered, *Never give up*.

I'm not writing this book because I've figured it all out. I'm writing it because I didn't quit, and because I believe you don't have to either. The road to where I am now was filled with failure, pain, uncertainty, and fear. I dropped out, and I got back up. I lost loved ones, and I questioned my own worth. I faced addiction, disappointment, and grief; yet, still I rose.

This book is for every person who's ever felt like giving up was easier than going on. It's for those who've watched doors close again and again, who've been underestimated, overlooked, or told they'd never amount to anything. It's for those who are tired of pretending not to care, when deep down they do. It's for you.

Along the way, I'll share my story, not to impress you, but to show you what's possible; and not just because I became a Commissioner or climbed a professional ladder, but because I faced the same storms you might be facing right now, and I found a way through. You will too.

We don't all start at the same place, we don't all get the same chances, but we do all get one life, one shot at writing our story; and no matter how many pages have been written in pain, *you get to write the rest in purpose*.

So before you go any further, I want you to know this:

You are not alone.

You never were.

And you don't have to ever give up.

With you on the journey,

Gary

# Front Acknowledgments

To my mentors and mentees—
You have helped shape the man I am, and the man I am still becoming.
Thank you for seeing in me what I couldn't always see in myself.
For your wisdom, your challenges, your guidance, and your belief.
You have each left an imprint on my journey.

To my family, friends, and colleagues—
Thank you for walking with me through every season.
For the words of encouragement, the hard truths, the prayers, the laughter, and the love.
You stood by me when I was finding my voice, and when I was learning to use it with purpose.
You reminded me—often and always—that I was never alone.

To my living siblings—Loretta, Diane, Angelique, and Jerome ("Romey")—thank you for your love, your presence, and your unwavering support. Each of you has held space for me in your own way, and I am deeply grateful to walk this life with you as family.

To those who've ever felt unseen—
This book is a light for you.
May you find your reflection in these pages.
May you feel hope rise.

And finally, to everyone who continues to believe in second chances, quiet courage, and the power of becoming—
Thank you for reminding the world that grace and greatness often walk hand in hand.


With humility and gratitude,
Gary P Jenkins

# PART I: ROOTS AND REALITY

*Where it starts doesn't determine where it ends.*

# Chapter 1: The World I Was Born Into

*Family dynamics, community, the unspoken rules of survival, and early loss.*

I was born last, the eighth child, the baby; and in some ways, the one who was supposed to carry the hope.

In my family, being the youngest didn't mean being spoiled. It meant inheriting everything—the love and the loss, the pride and the pain, the expectations and the silences. It meant being born into a storm that started long before I arrived and being asked, silently and unfairly, to be the peace.

We grew up in a neighborhood where struggle wasn't a phase; rather, it was the ground we walked on. The streets taught us things school never did: how to read a face before it turned dangerous, how to talk without saying too much, how to disappear when necessary. The lessons were unwritten but urgent. Survival was the curriculum.

The world outside our home was loud—sirens, arguments, music, metal gates slamming shut. But the world inside our home was louder, and not always in volume, but in weight. There were days filled with laughter and dancing, and days where no one spoke. Days where someone was missing and no one explained why. We didn't ask. We just adjusted.

My mother had five children before she met my father. When we were born, he carried with him the burden of his addictions. He wasn't absent in theory, but he wasn't fully present either. He showed us glimpses of love, but he couldn't stay long enough to anchor us in it. I know he loved us in his own way; but love, without guidance or healing, can collapse under its own weight.

When he died, due in part to substance use, it wasn't just a loss; rather, a confirmation of a fear I hadn't yet learned to name: that men in my world didn't last long, that fathers didn't stay, and that we, the children, would have to become the protectors, even before we were done being protected.

My mother became everything after that. She didn't have the luxury of time to grieve out loud. She had mouths to feed, children to guide, bills to avoid, and pain to swallow. I watched her hands, how they moved constantly, stirring pots, braiding hair, scrubbing floors, folding laundry. Her body was a machine for love; and like many Black mothers in this country, her labor was invisible and infinite.

She held our family together with threads of willpower, even when those threads were fraying. We had very little in material terms, but she gave us what she could: discipline, warmth, and dignity. And though the world outside told us we were poor, she made sure we never felt worthless.

I used to watch her from the hallway as she sat in the kitchen, sometimes staring into space, other times humming to herself. I wondered what memories she carried, what dreams she sacrificed to raise us. We never really talked about her dreams, for that was a luxury reserved for other people.

We had eight children in our home, each of us navigating our own storm. Some of my siblings got caught in the winds—incarceration, addiction, despair. Others found their own quiet resistance: music, church, escape. For me, it was observing, watching, and taking mental notes. I was trying to make sense of the chaos.

One of my sisters, one I never got to know, died at just sixteen. I was an infant. Her name was spoken in quiet reverence, and her absence was a constant presence. She became a kind of legend in our family. The one who had promise, the one who was lost too soon; and even though I never met her, I felt the pressure of her memory, as if I had to live not just for me, but for her too.

Then there was Loretta.

Loretta was fourteen years older than me, and more than a sister, she was a second mother, a protector, a visionary. She saw something in me I couldn't see in myself yet. She told me I didn't have to be like the others, that I could be more, and that I should be more. It wasn't that she dismissed our family—she loved them fiercely; but she knew that the cycle had to break somewhere, and she quietly, powerfully decided it would break with me.

She would sit with me after school and ask what I learned. She would talk to me about college like it was inevitable. She didn't coddle me, she called me up. She reminded me that I wasn't my surroundings, even when they screamed otherwise; and the most radical thing she gave me was expectation. She expected me to rise, and because of that, I began to believe I could.

The streets outside didn't believe in dreams. They believed in shortcuts, in fast money, and in running before you get caught. I watched friends disappear into systems—juvenile detention, group homes, eventually prison. I saw some of them come back different, harder, angrier, and emptier; and I wondered, Why not me?

There's no easy answer, but part of it was the fire I had; and part of it was that people like Loretta kept fanning it.

Growing up, I saw things no child should have to process: drug overdoses, violent arrests, families evicted in the middle of winter. I learned how to numb myself to pain before I ever learned algebra; and yet, I also saw love, I saw neighbors who shared groceries when cupboards were bare, and I saw laughter erupt during the darkest nights. I saw joy—not the kind you buy, but the kind you build out of survival.

People would sometimes say I had "potential." That word followed me around like a shadow. Teachers, mentors, even strangers would say it. "You've got potential;" and for a while, I resented it, for potential without opportunity feels like a curse. It's like telling someone they could fly while keeping them locked in a cage.

Still, I held onto those words. I didn't always believe them, but I held them close. I thought, Maybe they see something I don't, and that "maybe" became a seed, one I watered quietly with every good decision, every escape from a bad influence, every night I studied instead of going out, and every time I walked away from a fight.

We didn't talk about mental health in my house. We didn't use words like depression or anxiety; yet, I had them, I carried them like invisible weights, and there were days I felt like I was drowning, and no one even noticed. Nonetheless, I learned how to smile through it, how to move through pain, and how to function, for in my world, emotions were a luxury. You couldn't afford to break down when survival demanded you stand up.

And yet, I remember the moments I almost gave up.

Moments when the pressure felt like it would crush me, when I felt like I was failing everyone who believed in me, and when I looked around and thought, What's the point of all this? Those were the moments when I'd sit in silence, close my eyes, and hear a whisper from somewhere deep inside: Never give up.

I didn't know where that voice came from. Maybe God, maybe Loretta, maybe the version of me I hadn't yet become; but I listened, and that voice became my anchor.

Eventually, I started saying it out loud. First quietly, then louder, until "never give up" became not just a mantra, but a mission.

That mission became the foundation of my life. I wasn't just trying to escape poverty. I was trying to make meaning out of it. To rise, not in spite of my past, but because of it.

So yes, I was born into struggle, into a family stitched together by survival, an into a world that wasn't always kind, fair, or forgiving; but I was also born into something else: love, Purpose, Fire.

The world I was born into didn't break me, it built me, and even in its harshest lessons, it gave me everything I needed to begin the journey toward who I was meant to become.

Because I was never just born into the hood.

I was born into a story worth telling.

And that story starts here.

There were other moments that shaped me, small, often forgotten details that left a permanent imprint. Like the day I got into a fight at school, and I was maybe ten. A boy had said something about my mother—crude, disrespectful, and I lost it, I swung hard, and blood ran down his lip. The teacher pulled us apart, and I sat in the principal's office, trembling, not just from the fight, but from what I knew would come next.

When I got home, Loretta didn't yell. She sat me down and asked, "What did he say?" I told her. She nodded. "You're not wrong for defending your mother," she said. "But you've got to be smarter. You've got more to lose than he does."

That stuck with me. Even at ten years old, I understood what she meant. When you grow up in a neighborhood like mine, your margin for error is smaller. You can't afford to be reckless. You can't afford to be caught slipping, because when you fall, the systems don't catch you, they punish you.

That understanding made me cautious, but also strategic. I became someone who watched, who calculated, who waited for the right time to act. I learned how to move in a room full of tension. I learned how to sense danger before it arrived, and I learned how to speak when it mattered.

Eventually, these skills would help me navigate the professional world; but at the time, they just helped me survive.

The memories are vivid—my brother coming home from jail and trying to readjust to a world that didn't wait for him. My sister working two jobs and still not making ends meet. My mother crying quietly when she thought no one could hear. My own heart pounding when the police drove down our block slowly, windows half-rolled, eyes scanning every face.

And yet, we lived.

We loved.

We celebrated birthdays with dollar store balloons and hand-made cakes. We had cookouts in the summer and watched fireworks on rooftops. We danced in our socks across the linoleum floor. We sang, we forgave, and we kept going.

Sometimes I wonder how we did it, how my mother didn't collapse under the weight, and how Loretta managed to be a sister, mother, mentor, and friend without ever once asking for a thank-you. Sometimes I wonder how I found the strength to believe there was something else out there for me.

I then realize, it wasn't strength alone, it was purpose.

Even as a child, I had the sense that I wasn't just surviving for myself; rather, I was carrying something forward, a legacy, a message, a chance; and that belief became a lifeline.

There were nights when I lay in bed and whispered to myself, "One day," One day, you'll have your own place. One day, you'll sit behind a desk with your name on the door. One day, your story will matter.

I didn't know then what that would look like, but I held onto the vision, and I repeated it to myself like scripture. One day.

Now, looking back, I see how many people played a role in keeping that day within reach.

There was Mrs. Chislom, my 4th grade teacher, who pulled me aside and said, "You're smart. Don't waste it." There was the older guy on the block who told me, "Go home, little man. This ain't for you," when I lingered near something I shouldn't have seen. There was the neighborhood guy who offered to pay my book fees when I started college.

And there was Loretta—always Loretta—watching over me like a second spine.

That's the thing about resilience. It doesn't grow in isolation, it grows in community, in glances, gestures, affirmations, interventions; and in all the ways people quietly say: I believe in you.

If you're reading this, maybe no one ever said that to you. Or maybe they did, but you didn't believe it. Let me say it now, clearly and fully:

I believe in you.

Not because I know you. But because I know what's possible.

Because I've seen what can come from the most unlikely places.

Because I've lived the miracle of turning wounds into wisdom.

Because I know the world we are born into is not the end of the story—it's just the prologue.

And if there's one truth I carry from my earliest days until now, it's this:

Where you start does not determine where you finish.

# Chapter 2 – The Ones Who Tried Their Best

*Your father's legacy, your mother's sacrifices, your siblings' influence—and the role of generational struggle.*

There is a story we carry, not always spoken, but embedded in the bones. A story of the ones who came before us, the ones who tried, often quietly, often painfully, to do their best. Some survived, some broke, while some passed on the same pain they never had the tools to name; and yet, here we are.

We are the inheritors of their decisions, their silences, their resilience, and their regrets. However, with that inheritance comes a choice: repeat the patterns or rewrite the story.

This chapter is for the ones who wanted to do better but didn't know how.

It's for the parent who yelled but didn't know they were echoing generations of unheard rage. It is for the caregiver who worked too much and loved too little, not because they didn't care, but because they were never shown how.

It's for the teacher who saw your pain but didn't know how to ask, the social worker who burned out trying to fix what was never theirs to carry, the neighbor who looked away because they, too, had wounds they were hiding.

It's for the ones who were present but not whole; and for the ones who survived but never healed.

They tried, and sometimes, trying looks messy.

Trying looks like staying in a job that drains the soul because there's a child who needs food on the table. It looks like saying "no" too often because "yes" feels dangerous. It looks like overprotection, under-affection, fear disguised as control, and silence mistaken for strength.

And it also looks like prayer.

It looks like showing up when it's hard, like crying in the bathroom so no one sees, and like tucking in children while holding back the storm within.

It looks like hiding the pills, hiding the tears, hiding the truth, because nobody taught them that the truth could set them free.

They were not perfect.

But they were not monsters either.

They were people trying to make it in a world that gave them no map and no rest.

Now, many of us sit in therapy, in healing circles, in silence, trying to piece together the fragments they left behind, trying to understand how love could hurt, and how pain could feel familiar, and how we became fluent in self-denial because that's what they spoke at home.

We grieve, and we also honor, for trying matters, because effort, even when flawed, deserves to be remembered, and because we cannot heal what we do not acknowledge.

When it comes to me, I used to wonder how much pain a person could carry before they broke. For in my family, breaking wasn't an option. There was no backup plan, no safety net, no cavalry coming. As such, everyone held it in, compressed it, and tucked it away beneath their chores, their duties and their daily grind. They didn't cry in public, and they didn't say "I'm struggling;" rather, they said, "I'm fine," and kept it moving.

That's what survival looked like. It was the art of holding on, even when everything begged you to let go. Yet holding on isn't the same as healing; and that's the part of the story I want to make sure is told, because it's one thing to admire strength, and it's another to examine what it costs.

Several family member's health began to decline when I was in high school. The years of stress, malnutrition, and lack of rest had done their damage. We didn't talk about it much, as it was just another thing to be managed, and another burden to fold into the day. But I remember for example how my own mother started moving slower. Her hands shook more, she needed help getting up the stairs, and still, she cooked, still, she folded our laundry, and still, she said, "God is good."

That was her anchor, her way of pushing back against a world that told her she didn't matter. Faith, not in systems or people, but in something bigger, something unbreakable, and I didn't understand it fully then, but I do now. Faith wasn't just belief; rather, it was defiance.

Loretta saw it too, but she responded differently.

While my mother turned inward, Loretta turned outward. She read books, attended workshops, and started talking to other women in the community about stress, trauma, and healing. She was ahead of her time, talking about "intergenerational wounds" before that was a thing people said.

I think she knew that survival wasn't enough. That we needed something more.

She used to tell me, "Just because someone gave you pain, doesn't mean you have to pass it on." That stayed with me, and it still does.

Loretta tried her best not to pass it on.

And I think that's what makes someone a healer, not that they've never been hurt, but that they refuse to let their hurt define the future.

She didn't go to social work school, she didn't become a therapist, but she became my first example of what it means to interrupt a cycle, to break the silence, and to choose something different.

And in doing so, she gave me permission to do the same.

It didn't happen all at once. I still had my own battles, but still had to unlearn the lessons of the street—"don't feel," "don't trust," "don't need." But Loretta's quiet guidance was like a whisper in the background, reminding me that there was another way to live.

Even when I didn't listen, she stayed.

Even when I messed up, she stayed.

There's power in that kind of consistency; and in a world where people disappear, the ones who stay become sacred.

I also need to say this: not everyone who tried their best did it well.

There were adults in my life who made terrible decisions. They lashed out instead of talking. They hurt me because they were hurting; and I used to carry so much anger about that.

But over time, I've come to understand that people can be both broken and trying. They can be both damaging and loving; and they can be both lost and still guiding others home.

That doesn't excuse harm, but it does make space for complexity and for humanity; and when I look back now, I see that most of the people in my story didn't get what they needed when they were young. They were parenting without being parented. They were loving without being loved, and they were hoping without having ever seen hope modeled. And still, they tried. For example, I think about my uncle sometimes, the one who drank too much and shouted too loud, and the one who slammed doors and scared the kids. I used to think he was the villain in our story; but then I learned more.

He never got help, and never had someone sit him down and say, "You deserve to heal."

So he carried it. And it leaked.

Pain, when not healed, doesn't just stay inside. It finds ways out through anger, through silence, through distance, through overwork and through under-love.

That's why this work matters. That's why telling these stories matters.

Because someone has to say, "It stops here."

Someone has to look at the patterns and say, "I see you. I name you. And I'm not repeating you."

That's the work of repair.

And it's the most courageous work there is.

When I started doing my own healing, I didn't know where to begin. There was no manual for "how to undo decades of generational trauma." No checklist. No one right way. But I knew I had to start.

So I did something radical: I started telling the truth.

At first, just to myself.

Then, slowly, to others.

I admitted that I was tired. That I was angry. That I was scared. That I didn't want to be strong all the time. That I wanted softness, connection, peace.

I admitted that I was human.

And that's when things began to shift.

I joined groups. At first, I barely spoke. I just listened, but even that was medicine. To hear other people say out loud the things I had buried deep, there was power in that.

And eventually, I spoke too.

Spoke about my fears, my guilt, my grief, an my dreams.

And every time I did, the shame lessened, and the weight lifted.

I wish the ones who tried their best could've had that. Could've known what it felt like to be seen without judgment, to be loved without conditions, and to be held without having to hold everything together.

But maybe, in some way, they live through me.

Maybe every time I choose healing, I'm honoring their struggle, giving their pain a purpose, and turning their survival into my freedom.

And maybe that's the point.

Not to blame, not to forget, but to build on what they gave, and to take their "trying" and transform it into thriving.

This chapter is for them.

The mothers who worked three jobs and never complained.

The fathers who didn't know how to say "I love you" but showed up anyway.

The siblings who protected each other when no one else would.

The neighbors who cooked extra so no one went hungry.

The elders who prayed even when the world gave them nothing to believe in.

They weren't perfect, but they were persistent.

They didn't always get it right, but they refused to give up.

And in a world designed to break them, they held each other together with threadbare hands and unbreakable hope.

They tried their best, that's worth remembering, and now it's your turn.

# Chapter 3 – The Gift and Grief of Big Sisters

*How Loretta, Ida, and the Memory of the Sister You Never Knew Shaped You*

Let me tell you something that might surprise you: sometimes, the people who shape us the most are the ones we knew only for a moment, and the ones who never left our side. This chapter is about both.

It's about Loretta, the sister who stood like a lighthouse in your storm. And it's about Ida, the sister whose name was a whisper, a question, a longing, and a mystery. One protected you in life, the other left before you had a chance to understand what protection even meant, and both have lived in you, walked beside you, shaped your steps, even when you didn't realize it.

Let's start with Loretta.

Loretta was everything a big sister could be and more. She was brave, bold, and watchful, and she was your armor in a world you didn't yet know how to navigate. When the world was confusing, she explained it, when it was dangerous, she guarded you, and when it was cruel, she softened the blow. Loretta was the one who could see the storm coming before you even heard thunder. She didn't just stand in the way of harm; rather, she taught you how to find your own strength, gently, firmly, and quietly.

She carried a kind of wisdom you didn't know how to name then; but you do now.

And yet, for all her strength, there was tenderness. You remember how she brushed your hair back behind your ears when you were too upset to speak; and how she squeezed your shoulder before you walked into school, like a secret message saying, "You've got this."

Loretta made you feel like there was always someone in your corner, someone always watching your back, and someone always who saw you, not just as a child to be protected, but as a person in the making; and that belief, the one she had in you, became the foundation of the belief you started to have in yourself.

Now let's talk about Ida.

You didn't get to grow up with her. You didn't get bedtime stories or inside jokes. Ida was the sister who died too young, the sister whose presence hovered like a hush in the room. You could feel her absence, thick and sacred, and you could see it in your parents' eyes when they thought no one was looking. You could also feel it in the silence that sometimes settled over dinner.

No one taught you how to grieve someone you barely met; but somehow, you grieved her.

You imagined her laugh, you wondered what her advice would have been, and you constructed a relationship in dreams, in fragments, and in questions. That's when you then began to understand something essential: memory doesn't depend on time; rather, it depends on love.

Psychologists call this "symbolic immortality." It's how we carry those we've lost in our daily lives, in rituals, in habits, in stories, and in dreams. Ida then became a part of your moral compass, a reason to do better, to be better, and to live more fully; and sometimes, you caught yourself living for both of you, for you became the sibling who stayed, who survived, and who had to make sense of two roles: the protected and the remembering.

And it was not easy.

Because grief is a shapeshifter. It's not just sadness; rather, it's also responsibility, it's guilt, and it's wondering if you would've been the same person had she lived. It's asking yourself if your parents would've looked at you differently, or raised you differently.

But then there's this: you are exactly who you are because of both of them.

Loretta showed you how to protect others. Ida taught you how to honor the sacredness of every moment.

Loretta gave you presence. Ida gave you depth.

Loretta showed you how to speak up. Ida taught you the power of quiet reflection.

Loretta gave you strength. Ida gave you sensitivity.

And both gave you love.

So when you advocate for someone who's overlooked... when you speak truth in a room full of silence... when you refuse to turn your back on someone in pain... you're living out what they gave you, both of them, in different ways, and in layered, complex, and beautiful ways.

This chapter of your life is not just a story of sisters. It's a story of integration.

We often think we have to choose between remembering and moving forward; but what if it's both? What if moving forward is remembering differently?

Loretta and Ida are not just parts of my past; rather, they are part of my foundation. Loretta with her protective presence, Ida with her guiding absence; and one held my hand, while the other held my heart.

And I walk forward with both.

And that has been my offering, my testimony, and my strength; and I invite you to draw inspiration in that to remind yourself as needed that you're not alone, and you never were.

# PART II: THE STORM AND THE STAND

*Trying to make it out, when no one expects you to.*

# Chapter 4 – Growing Up in the Shadows:

*Violence, Drugs, Incarceration—and Your First Glimpses of Something More*

There's a story that doesn't get told often enough, and it is the one about the child who walks to school past chalk outlines, needles in the gutter, and corner boys who never got a second chance. It is the one about growing up in the shadows of the system, behind barred windows and broken promises, where you learn too young what survival means, and too late that it doesn't always mean living.

You know that story. You lived it.

You grew up in a world where your first lessons weren't from books; rather, they were from watching, watching your uncle disappear into a cell, watching your neighbor nod out on the stoop, and watching your mother cry behind closed doors. They were also from watching your friends get harder every year, until even laughter started to sound like pain.

And somehow, through all that watching, you started to see something else.

Let's be honest: survival isn't just instinct; rather, it's a kind of genius. It's reading the room before you walk into it, it's knowing which blocks are safe at what hour, and it's feeling the shift in the air before the sirens start. Survival is also figuring out, sometimes in silence, that you want something more, even if you don't know what "more" means yet.

But, you weren't supposed to make it, and not because you weren't smart, and not because you weren't capable; but because the math was against you, and statistics predicted your fall before you even learned to ride a bike.

One in three Black boys born in the U.S. today can expect to be incarcerated in his lifetime if current trends continue, and that's not fate; rather, that's policy, that's environment, and that's systems doing what they were designed to do.

And yet, you began to imagine something different.

It wasn't a lightning bolt moment; rather, it was gradual, it was a teacher who didn't give up on you, a book that lit something up inside you, and a stranger's kindness. It was a relative's warning, and a dream you couldn't name but couldn't shake.

That's what this chapter is about, and not just the pain, but the possibility, and not just the shadows, but the sparks.

Because you weren't just trying to survive; rather, you were trying to become.

You started to recognize that the streets weren't the whole story, and that your environment was shaping you, but it didn't have to define you; and that even in the darkest alleys, there's light leaking through the cracks. Sometimes the crack is a poem, sometimes it's a conversation, and sometimes it's a question that won't leave you alone.

"Is this all there is?"

That's the question that changes everything.

I never asked to be born into the shadows, yet shadows are not just the absence of light; rather, they are the presence of things that block it. In the neighborhood I grew up in, there were many things blocking the light, drugs, violence, incarceration, and silence. There was also a dangerous kind of expectation, one that said, "You won't make it out."

I remember the first time I heard gunshots. I was four. The sound didn't shake me. It was more like punctuation, and something final. I had been playing outside with my cousins, and Loretta called us in before the sirens came. She always knew the signs. There was a sixth sense about her, a knowing that came from watching too many people fall through cracks that weren't supposed to exist in the first place.

The blocks I grew up on weren't in the travel brochures. We didn't have playgrounds; rather, we had cracked sidewalks and corner stores where people didn't buy food; rather, escape. I saw too much, too young: the quiet deals, the men who disappeared and came back changed, and the mothers trying to smile through a grief they never named. However, I didn't know it was trauma, for I thought it was just life.

At school, teachers didn't expect much from us. We were numbers, names to be memorized until the end of June. The special ones, those rare, burning souls who tried to see us, usually didn't last long. They either got disillusioned or transferred to schools where children didn't flinch when someone yelled in the hallway.

And yet, somehow, even in all of that, I glimpsed something more.

It wasn't a big thing, it wasn't a vision or a bolt of lightning; rather, it was small, subtle, a feeling, and a conversation. The look in a stranger's eyes who once told me, "You're smart. You know that, right?" I didn't believe them, but I remembered; and remembering, in a place built on forgetting, is its own kind of miracle.

There were books, old ones, torn ones, and Loretta had a way of bringing them home. She'd find them at the thrift store, the church basement, or sometimes just left behind on the train. She'd press them into my hand and say, "Read it. You never know." And I didn't know, but I read them anyway.

That's how I met James Baldwin, Langston Hughes, Malcolm and Maya and Audre and Toni. Their words burned a hole in the darkness. They didn't save me, not yet, but they reminded me that people who

45

looked like me had done more than just survive. They had built, written, led,  and dreamed; and somehow, just by knowing that, I began to imagine I could too.

Still, the streets had a rhythm, and it was easier to move with the beat than to stand still and question the music. My friends were getting caught up, some in the game, some in the system,  and some in both. The line between "them" and "me" was thinner than anyone wants to admit. I wasn't better, I was just lucky, and Loretta, always Loretta, watching, intervening, lying if she had to, and praying when nothing else worked.

There were days I hated her for it, for trying to keep me out of things, and for treating me like I was different, for I didn't want to be different, I wanted to belong; and looking back, I see what she saw: That my longing to belong could be the very thing that broke me.

We don't talk enough about the seduction of street life, the pride, the community, or the code. It gives you an identity, a sense of power in a world where you often feel invisible; and for young Black boys who grow up in the shadows, power, even if it's borrowed, it is magnetic.

But so is purpose.

And it was purpose, not fear, that eventually pulled me away.

The first real moment came the day my cousin got locked up. He was like a brother to me, and we were inseparable. I looked up to him, as he had charm, confidence, and everyone knew his name. However, one day, just like that, he was gone. A raid, a sentence, and a future wiped out by a few decisions and a system that was already waiting.

I visited him once, behind the glass, and he wouldn't look me in the eye. I didn't cry then, but I couldn't stop thinking about what he said: "Don't be like me." That was all; but it was enough.

46

It planted something, not a seed, but more like a splinter, and a painful reminder that I had to find another way, even if I didn't know what that looked like.

There were mentors, eventually, but in those early days, it was mostly inner whispers, a quiet voice saying, "Keep going," a sense that someone—maybe God, maybe my grandmother's prayers—was carrying me. For I wasn't strong, not yet at least; but I was just determined not to die without trying.

If you've ever grown up in the shadows, you know what I mean. You know the ache. The tension between loyalty to your people and responsibility to yourself. You know what it means to carry the weight of "making it out" while still loving those who didn't.

You know the survivor's guilt.

But you also know the fire, the hunger, and the dreams you never told anyone, because even speaking them felt like betrayal. You know what it means to walk through your neighborhood like a ghost, already halfway gone in your mind, building a world no one else can see.

And if you don't know, then I hope you believe us.

Because there are so many of us, dreamers, fighters, broken and brilliant, growing up in the shadows and still searching for the light.

This is where the story truly begins, and not in triumph; rather, in tragedy and in tension.

The tension of who you are, and who you might become.

And it is in that tension that the real transformation starts.

# Chapter 5—Almost Giving Up (But Didn't)

*SUNY Oswego. Failing. Leaving. Returning. Questionning everything—but choosing to stay the course.*

You almost didn't go back. Let's start there.

Because for a moment, it felt like everything had come undone. The grades, the pressure, the disillusionment. SUNY Oswego wasn't just a campus anymore; rather, it was a mirror, and what you saw staring back at you wasn't clear. You were unraveling in a place that was supposed to mean arrival.

And no one talks enough about that.

No one talks about what it feels like to walk away from a dream, and not because you don't want it, but because you're not sure if you belong in it anymore; and not because you're lazy or ungrateful or "not ready," but because somewhere along the way, the ground shifted under you and no one told you how to keep standing.

So you left, quietly, maybe even shamefully, and maybe no one asked why.

But the thing about leaving is: it makes you confront the parts of yourself you tried to outrun. When the noise dies down and the books are closed, you're left with the questions that never stopped whispering.

"Am I enough?"

"Can I really do this?"

"Was this a mistake?"

Those questions don't kill you; rather, they do something else, they scrape you raw, and they force you to decide who you are when no one is watching.

48

And that's where you started to remember, and not everything, not all at once, but little fragments of why you started. The moments you felt seen, the dreams that used to move you, the fire, flickering under the fatigue, and the thought that maybe, just maybe, you weren't done yet

Do I go back?

At first, the answer was no. For it was too hard, too painful, and too risky. You told yourself you were protecting yourself. But deep down, something stirred, because the absence didn't make you feel safe; rather, it made you feel unfinished.

There were glimpses, memories, and fragments, a professor's words, lingering, a class where something finally clicked, and a moment in the library, holding a book that felt like a key. There was a conversation that opened your eyes, and then there were the deeper things, the reasons you started this journey in the first place, and not to prove something to the world, but to yourself.

You hadn't lost the dream. You had just lost your way.

And so you returned, not with bravado, not with everything figured out, but with something far more powerful: resolve. A quiet, defiant decision to stay the course, to take one more step, then another, even when it hurt, and especially when it hurt.

And the work was still hard, the fear didn't evaporate, and the pressure remained; but this time, you were different, because you weren't running anymore; rather, you were building, slowly and intentionally.

You showed up for class, even on the days you didn't feel worthy of the seat.

You walked into the library and opened the books, even when the words blurred.

You asked for help. You listened. You re-learned how to believe.

you then started to win, and not in big, dramatic ways, but in small, compounding victories. A passed exam, a meaningful discussion, a professor who saw your growth, and a friend who said, "I'm proud of you." Each one like a rung on a ladder out of the doubt.

And you learned that success is not a straight line, and it's not perfection; rather, it's persistence.

You learned that failure isn't the opposite of progress; rather, it's part of it; and that leaving doesn't mean quitting forever. Sometimes it's a necessary pause, sometimes it's how you find your footing; but returning, that's where the transformation lives.

You earned your place, not by never falling, but by choosing to rise. Again and again.

That decision changed the trajectory of your life. SUNY Oswego became more than a campus. It became a crucible, a place where the old you burned away so the real you could emerge.

You began to notice things. How many other students were struggling silently. How many others felt like impostors. How many never returned after falling; and your heart started to change.

You began to understand: your story wasn't just yours. It was part of something bigger, a shared ache, and a shared hope.

That's when mentorship started calling to you. You didn't know it then, but your own journey was planting seeds of leadership, seeds of empathy, and seeds of purpose.

But we'll get to that in the next chapter.

For now, let this stand as a moment, and one that almost broke you, one that nearly stole your path, and one that taught you:

Resilience is not about avoiding the fall; rather, it's about getting up, remembering who you are, and walking forward with no guarantee— only courage.

This is the story of almost giving up.

But didn't.

# Chapter 6 – Mentors, Mirrors, and Moments That Matter

*Those who believed in you. The unexpected guides. Why mentorship changes everything—and why you still felt alone.*

Let's be honest: you didn't make it here alone; and no one ever does.

But isn't it strange how you can be surrounded by people who believe in you, who pour into you, who push you forward; yet you still feel utterly, terrifyingly alone?

That's the paradox of mentorship.

There were those who came into your life like whispers; and not grand entrances, and not loud declarations; but just quiet, and deliberate presence. There were professors, counselors, advisors, and elders in the community. Some looked like you, while some didn't; and some had walked your path, while others had studied it; but all of them gave you something you didn't even realize you needed: a mirror.

You didn't always recognize the moment as pivotal, it wasn't always a long conversation or some sit-down life coaching session; and often, it was just a comment scribbled in the margin of your paper:

"You have a voice. Don't let it get buried."

Perhaps it was a look across a crowded room when you spoke up for the first time in class, and someone nodded—as if to say, "Yes. You're allowed to be here."

There was the campus supervisor who saw how you handled conflict with care and said, "You're a leader, you know that?" Or the faculty member who stayed late after class to ask if you were okay—not because your grade depended on it, but because they sensed something was off.

And there was the advisor who asked the question that changed the course of everything:

"Have you ever thought about graduate school?"

You hadn't. Not seriously. Until that moment.

Here's what no one tells you: Mentorship can surround you, uplift you, even champion you—and still, there's a voice inside that refuses to be quiet.

That voice says,

"They must not really know you."

"If they saw how you think about yourself, they'd take it all back."

"You're a fraud. You're not like them."

Even when someone believes in you, it doesn't guarantee you'll believe in yourself. Even when a mentor opens a door, it doesn't mean you'll feel worthy enough to walk through it.

You carried your own doubts like bricks in a backpack, and those bricks weren't placed there by chance; rather, they came from years of hearing you were "too much" or "not enough." They came from years of navigating systems that weren't built for you, by people who never had to worry about code-switching or scholarship deadlines or how to explain to your family what you're even studying.

Sometimes, the most profound mentorship came not in formal settings, but in the margins of your life.

An older student who shared their notes and told you not to drop that class because "the first few weeks are always rough." The cafeteria worker who smiled every morning and called you "baby" like you were theirs. The custodian who saw you crying in the hallway and handed you a tissue without asking questions.

They didn't have official titles; rather, they mentored you in resilience, and not in belonging, but in not giving up.

Sometimes that mentorship came from books—Audre Lorde, James Baldwin, bell hooks. Writers who named your experience when no one else could. They said what you were afraid to say, they told the truth, they didn't sugarcoat the cost of becoming, and you read their words like sacred scripture.

But even with all that guidance, the ache never left. The ache of being in between.

Between the world you came from and the one you were entering. Between being celebrated in the classroom and misunderstood at home. Between moments of visibility and hours of invisibility.

You'd go home for break and find yourself code-switching without even thinking about it. You stopped talking about certain classes because your excitement was met with silence, or confusion, or worse—resentment.

You weren't trying to leave anyone behind, but you were growing, and sometimes growth feels like betrayal.

Even in the most affirming mentorship spaces, you often found yourself smiling politely, hiding the depth of your fatigue, your fear, and your fury, for it's hard to articulate the loneliness of being the first, or the only.

And yet… you still remember the turning points; and not the moment your mentor believed in you, but the moment you believed they might be right.

Maybe it was the time they asked you to lead a group project because they saw how others listened when you spoke. Or the time they handed you an application for a national fellowship and said, "You should go for this." Or the way they said your name with pride when introducing you at an event.

It was never just about academic achievement. It was about identity, voice, and worth.

Little by little, their belief began to seep into your cracks, and you started to sit up straighter. You started to trust your instincts, and to imagine a future you had never dared speak aloud.

That's the power of mentorship when it works. It doesn't overwrite your wounds, but it tells you: your wounds are not the end of the story.

And then it happened. One day, someone came to you.

Maybe it was a first-year student who asked if you could help with their résumé. Or a friend who wanted to talk about dropping out. Or someone from back home who said, "How did you do it?"

And just like that, you realized: You were becoming the very person you once needed.

Not perfectly, not always consciously, but naturally, for when you survive something, part of your healing is helping others survive it too.

You began to hold space, you began to affirm others' voices, and you began to reflect what had once been reflected to you.

That's the beautiful irony of mentorship:

We start by receiving it.

We grow by believing it.

We become whole by giving it away.

Your story is not just a timeline of degrees and jobs and accomplishments. It's a story of interruption, of someone stepping into your path and saying, "There's more for you," and of someone seeing what you could be before you could even name it.

And now you do that for others.

You see the student who sits in the back of the class. You notice the hesitation in their voice. You recognize the way they lower their eyes; because you were them.

And when you say, "I see you. I've been there," something opens.

Mentorship is not just a strategy; rather, it's a form of justice, and it's how we make the world less lonely, one reflection at a time.

One day, long after the late nights and library sessions, someone will say to you:

"Thank you for believing in me."

And you'll feel your throat tighten, because you'll remember how hard it was to believe in yourself.

And then you'll smile, because you'll realize: you did believe, eventually, for someone believed first.

That's the legacy.

The people who helped you see yourself, and the person you became because of it.

This chapter is for them. And this chapter is for you; because you were never as alone as you felt; but you were always as powerful as they saw you to be.

And now? You see it too.

# PART III: THE CLIMB

*Each rung on the ladder told me: Never give up.*

# Chapter 7 – Entering Public Service
*Early work for the city. Why DSS mattered. What it meant to serve.*

Public service didn't begin with a grand vision. It didn't come with a title, a press release, or a congratulatory post on LinkedIn. It began in the quiet, often invisible moments—those choices you made when no one was looking, no one was applauding, and no one quite knew how much it cost you to say yes.

The Department of Social Services (DSS) wasn't glamorous. The office lighting was harsh. The chairs were old, and the waiting rooms were crowded. Yet, something about it felt alive, urgent, and unfinished.

You walked in, not with certainty, but with curiosity, and a sense that maybe this work could matter, and maybe you could matter through this work.

At first, it was overwhelming. You were given forms, protocols, a desk, and very little training. The caseloads were astronomical, the phones rang off the hook, and people came in angry, afraid, or both. And still, you stayed, you sat across from them—mothers and fathers, seniors and teenagers, people with nowhere else to go—and you listened.

You learned to decode the system the way one learns a new language—through immersion, through mistakes, and through sheer necessity. What you then began to understand, almost immediately, was that the system wasn't built to be navigated by the people who needed it most. It was a maze—one that demanded patience, persistence, and often privilege. You then realized that your job wasn't just to process paperwork; rather, it was to help people survive the maze.

That changed everything.

## More Than a Job: A Call to Witness

DSS wasn't just a workplace. It was a frontline in the quiet battle for human dignity. You began to see behind the numbers—the human lives at stake. A child's lunch depended on a form being submitted in time. A father's housing voucher depended on a system that didn't crash that day; and a senior's medication coverage depended on someone reading the small print; and you were that someone.

There was the woman who came in every month, trying to keep her benefits active, with three kids in tow and eyes that told you more than her words ever could. There was the man who barely spoke English, clutching a crumpled letter he didn't understand. You began to notice the cracks in the floor—where people fell through, where the safety net didn't catch them.

You didn't have a cape, but you had a computer, a phone, a signature; and sometimes, those things made the difference.

You then started asking better questions, you stopped assuming, and you paused before saying "no." You looked for the loopholes that could help someone, not hurt them; and you advocated, you pushed back, you asked supervisors to take another look, and you worked late.

This wasn't about being a hero. It was about being human.

## The Cost of Caring

Now, the work changed you, but it also took its toll.

You cried in the bathroom, you carried stories home in your chest, and you felt helpless. Some nights, you couldn't sleep—thinking of the woman who left your office with nothing but a number to call, and you wondered if she'd be okay.

You watched coworkers burn out, harden, detach, and you promised yourself you wouldn't become numb. You also learned that empathy requires boundaries, you learned to hold space without carrying the weight alone, and you learned to care deeply without falling apart daily.

Still, there were days it felt like nothing changed. The same crises came through the door, the same flaws in the system repeated themselves; and still, you showed up.

Because sometimes change isn't a revolution—it's a ripple.

### Learning to Lead Without Permission

You also didn't wait to be promoted to start leading; rather, you mentored new staff, you created better systems for intake, and you sat in meetings and asked the uncomfortable questions. You got curious about policy, you read beyond your job description, and you looked at citywide numbers, budget lines, and legislation.

And slowly, the lens widened.

You began to see how systemic failures were not accidents—they were often designs. And if they were designed, maybe they could be redesigned. You started to think like a policymaker, even if your title hadn't caught up.

DSS became your training ground.

You learned how to talk to people from every walk of life. You learned how to write clearly, speak persuasively, organize your thoughts in crisis; and you became both advocate and administrator, both counselor and clerk.

The real leadership wasn't in the hierarchy. It was in how you treated people, in how you chose integrity when no one was watching, and in how you carried the weight of systems with compassion and courage.

## Seeing Through the Lens of Service

"Service" sounds soft. But it is anything but.

To serve is to say, "I will stand here with you." It is to say, "Your struggle matters to me, even if I can't solve it." It is to choose inconvenience over comfort, and to slow down when everything around you is speeding up.

Service is sitting with someone who is angry and not meeting them with anger. It's pausing to explain a form, again, even when you have 20 others waiting. It's noticing the mother who hasn't eaten today, the elder who is confused by a letter, and the young man whose frustration is masking fear.

You started to serve not just with your time, but with your attention; and your presence became the thing that mattered most; and people noticed.

They told you.

They said, "Thank you for seeing me."

And sometimes, that was the only reward; but it was enough.

## When the System Breaks—and You Stay Anyway

Public service means working within a system you didn't design—and often disagree with. You saw policies that didn't work, rules that were outdated, and budget constraints that made no sense. You also felt the weight of injustice, not as a theory, but as a daily reality.

Still, you didn't leave.

Not because you agreed with it all, but because you believed in the people, you believed that change required insiders, and that reform required resistance from within.

So you became strategic. You learned how to write memos that moved things. You learned which supervisors would listen, and how to make a case. You also learned how to build coalitions across departments; and you became both bold and wise.

And you kept your heart intact; and that may be the greatest miracle of all.

**Moments That Shaped You**

There are moments you'll never forget.

The first time a resident said, "You're the first person who made me feel human in here."

The first time a colleague asked you to train them, not because they had to, but because they trusted you.

The time you stayed after hours to help a father reapply for SNAP, and he got it.

The time you refused to let a file get buried—and someone's life changed because of it.

These moments didn't go viral. They didn't make headlines. But they made meaning.

And they made you.

**The Beginning of a Bigger Mission**

Eventually, DSS was no longer just a job. It was a launchpad.

You began to see your role not just in the micro—but in the macro. You started thinking about policy change, about advocacy, about systemic redesign, and about leadership.

You didn't know it then, but your path was unfolding. The skills you gained—communication, empathy, strategy, advocacy, resilience— were becoming the foundation for something far bigger.

You began to dream differently.

Not about leaving public service, but about transforming it.

Not about climbing for your own sake, but about rising so you could pull others up.

And that—right there—was the turning point.

The moment you realized: You are not just in public service; rather, you are becoming a public servant.

There's a difference.

One is a role; while the other is an identity.

## You Were Built for This

Some days you still ask, "Why me?"

But the real question is: Why not you?

You've been in the rooms where no one listened. You've stood at the counters where people were dismissed, and you've felt the sting of systems that ignore the soul.

That's why your voice matters.

That's why your leadership matters.

That's why this work matters.

DSS didn't give you your calling. It revealed it.

You were always meant to stand in the gap, to build the bridge, and to remind people they matter; and not with speeches, and not with fanfare; but with eye contact, with dignity, and with presence.

# Chapter 8 – When You're Called to Lead

*The dream of becoming Commissioner. Declaring it at 22. Realizing it at 55.*

Some dreams aren't whispered; rather, they're declared; and you declared yours early.

You were 22 when you said it aloud for the first time: "I want to be Commissioner one day." It felt too big to speak and too sacred not to; but you didn't say it to impress anyone; rather, you said it to affirm something already alive inside of you.

Yes, you were 22 when you declared it—not to boast, not to perform, but to mark the moment your soul spoke. You said it with a fire that outran your fear, with clarity that defied your credentials, and with the quiet knowing that leadership was not something you would chase; rather, it was something you were born for.

There was no map, there were no promises; rather, there was just a calling; and calling doesn't care how young you are; rather, it only asks that you listen.

You were far from it then, for you didn't know the path, the politics, or the price; yet you knew the call, and that call stayed with you.

## The Path Was Never Straight

You weren't handed the keys and you weren't ushered to the front; rather, you earned every inch.

Through the chaos of bureaucracy, the heartbreak of broken systems, the agony of not-enough-resources-but-too-much-responsibility, you stayed, and not because it was easy, but because it was yours.

You showed up when others left, you spoke up when others stayed silent, you challenged what wasn't working, and you protected what was. You also made room for others to rise, even when you were still climbing.

And when people doubted you, overlooked you, underestimated you?

You let your work answer them, quietly, powerfully, and consistently.

**The Wait Wasn't a Delay. It Was Preparation**

And you didn't arrive at 55; rather, you became at 55.

Because becoming is what happens when you do the inner work no one sees.

The late-night questioning, the invisible labor of integrity, and doing the right thing when no one's watching: That's where the real becoming took place, and not in boardrooms, but in back rooms. You didn't just get the role; rather, you became the role; and the title didn't crown you; rather, it confirmed you.

Commissioner wasn't a surprise; rather, it was the natural unfolding of decades of alignment. You weren't new to power; rather, you had simply grown into its weight.

Leadership, you'd learn, wasn't about a title; rather, it was about vision, responsibility, and the willingness to stand when no one else would. It was about sleepless nights, tough calls, and holding the weight of decisions that affected thousands of lives.

Over the years, the dream never faded; rather, it evolved. You served in roles that stretched you, you saw systems from the inside, their inefficiencies, their buried brilliance, and their human cost. You built teams, you fixed what you could, you fought for what mattered, and you stayed, even when leaving would've been easier. You also brought dignity back into decision-making, humanity into policy, and empathy into execution. You remembered every waiting room, every intake form, every family you served when no one was looking. You never led from above. You led from within.

And you made sure that power never divorced itself from purpose. For, this is not the end of the road; rather, it's the deepening of the call. Furthermore, there is a kind of leadership that seeks the stage; and then there's the kind that seeks the soul.

You chose the latter; and you didn't climb to escape; rather, you climbed to transform, to build, and to mend. You climbed to reimagine what leadership could feel like, look like, and sound like.

You created tables where others had never been invited. You didn't just open doors—you held them open. You didn't just lead meetings—you led movements.

And , you didn't just fulfill a dream; rather, you fulfilled a responsibility to every 22-year-old who dares to dream big, for you were called and you answered.

And here's the miracle: You didn't wait to be ready; rather, you answered before the path was clear; and that's what leaders do.

They walk into rooms not because they feel qualified, but because they feel called. They speak truths that others bury; and they carry burdens that others avoid. They also build bridges where others burn them; and they rise without losing their roots.

You didn't just get the position; rather, you earned the trust of a system that rarely trusts. You earned the hope of those who had given up; and you earned your voice, and used it for others.

Legacy, then, is not a title; rather, it's a trace, for the title will come and go, but the people you lifted, the policies you rewrote, the minds you opened; and the hearts you healed: Those remain; and you will never fully know the ripple effect of your "yes."

You will never see every life that was changed because you stayed when you could've left. You told the truth when silence was safer; and you believed in the future when the present was a mess.

That's the mystery of true leadership: You don't need to see the full harvest to plant the seed; and to the One Who's Called to Lead—This Is Your Reminder

But being called to lead also meant being tested.

You were tested by setbacks, by people who didn't believe in you, by budgets that wouldn't budge and politics that played chess with people's lives. You were tested by your own doubts: "Am I enough?" "Is it too late?" "Do I belong in this room?"

And still, you rose.

By 55, the dream wasn't a fantasy; rather, it was a file with your name on it, a mantle placed, and a responsibility accepted.

Commissioner.

But the title didn't change you; rather, it revealed you. You didn't become someone new; rather, you became more of who you always were.

You never forgot the late nights at DSS, the policies you once challenged, or the mentors who lifted you. You never forgot the residents who trusted you, or the times you almost gave up—but didn't.

Commissioner was never the destination; rather, it was a continuation.

Because when you're truly called to lead, you never stop listening, you never stop growing, and you never forget where you came from.

This chapter of your life didn't begin at 55. It began the moment you chose to believe in the future version of you—the one you spoke into existence at 22.

You didn't just become Commissioner; rather, you fulfilled a calling, and not to chase power, but to become a force for healing.

You were 22 when you saw it.  You were 55 when you stepped into it.

But you were born for it. You were called.

And you answered.

# Chapter 9. Leadership from the Inside Out

*Empowering staff. Changing systems. Building trust. The unseen cost of visibility as a Black man in power.*

Leadership looks different when you carry history on your shoulders. It's not just about policies and meetings, org charts and strategy. It's also about being seen, and being watched. It's about walking into a room and knowing you're not just representing yourself, but you're also representing possibility, resilience, and, whether you asked for it or not, a whole community.

You didn't always want that responsibility, you accepted it; and when you stepped into leadership, you made a quiet vow to lead from the inside out. That meant doing the internal work, on your identity, your values, and your fears, so that your leadership could be authentic. You also knew the danger of leading from a mask, for you had seen the cost of pretending.

So, you chose something different.

You led by empowering, you met staff where they were, and you asked questions before offering solutions. You listened deeply, even when time was tight, you believed people were more than their job descriptions, and you fought to build systems that reflected that belief.

You created spaces where people felt seen, heard, valued, and where leadership wasn't a performance but a practice of presence.

You pushed for trauma-informed approaches, equity-driven policy, and leadership pipelines that included voices too often silenced. You challenged the status quo, not with fire, but with fierce integrity; and change followed.

But so did resistance, for not everyone wanted systems to change, and not everyone was ready for your kind of leadership. There were whispers, challenges, and microaggressions dressed in corporate language. You had to smile while being scrutinized, and you had to prove yourself twice as hard, knowing one mistake would echo louder because of who you were.

The cost of visibility was real.

Being a Black man in power meant walking a razor-thin line between strength and stereotype. If you were direct, you were "angry." If you were passionate, you were "too emotional," and if you were measured, you were "detached." There was no script to follow—just your own compass.

And still, you led.

You led with transparency, you brought others with you, you stayed accountable, and not just to goals, but to growth. You made space for others to rise, and in doing so, you multiplied your impact.

Inside, there were days of exhaustion, and of asking, "Why do I have to fight this hard just to lead with integrity?" But those moments passed, and in their place, came clarity.

You were never just leading an entity, but you were also modeling a new kind of leadership, one rooted in wholeness, truth, and justice.

And that's what people remember. They do not remember the press releases, or the accolades, but how they felt around you, empowered, capable, and called forward.

To lead from the inside out means beginning not with strategy, but with people. It means listening before directing. It means seeing potential before performance; and you learned this early, for early enough, you knew staff weren't disengaged; rather they were disillusioned. You knew they were not just ineffective, but just unheard. You didn't blame them for the symptoms of burnout, you, instead investigated the source. And when you led, you didn't demand loyalty, you cultivated it.

Empowerment wasn't a speech. It was shared decision-making. It was training with integrity, and not just compliance. It was investing in your staff's growth because you knew systems don't transform unless people do.

You sat with team members one by one, and you asked, "What's getting in the way of you doing your best work?"

Then you moved the barriers.

You didn't throw around the word "trust," you embodied it. You made space for questions, and for people to challenge you; and you didn't need to be the smartest in the room, you simply needed to be the most present.

Leadership from the inside out isn't always celebrated, but it's always felt, and it's how you made your mark, for true leadership never begins with a title. It begins with a reckoning, with a question, and with the quiet yet unrelenting whisper: "Will you carry the weight of this?"

For some, the journey into leadership is paved with encouragement and mentorship. For others, it's more like crossing a tightrope with the world watching and waiting for you to fall.

## Changing Systems

Systems are slow to change not because they're complex, but because they were built to protect the status quo. You understood that, you understood that systems are just people, rules, habits, and fears, codified and repeated. You didn't just want to tweak policy, you wanted to alter culture. You saw how outdated protocols silenced innovation, you saw how decisions made in isolation disempowered those closest to the front lines, and you saw how residents were treated like problems to manage instead of people to support.

So, you challenged those norms, and not with slogans, but with action. You formed cross-disciplinary teams, you invited dissenting voices to the table; and you ensured to prioritize both efficiency and dignity.

You didn't talk about trauma-informed care, you embedded it. Not just for clients, but for your staff, for they, too, carried invisible wounds. You then made emotional intelligence a competency, and you made rest and reflection part of the work week.

Changing systems meant you were often alone, but you weren't afraid of solitude; and you used it to think, to dream, and to reimagine what leadership could look like.

**Building Trust**

Trust isn't built in town halls; rather, it's built in hallways, in quiet moments, and in consistency.

You kept your word, you showed up, and you said "I don't know" when you didn't. You took responsibility when things went wrong, and you gave credit when things went right.

Staff began to believe again, not just in the mission, but also in themselves, and not just in the work, but also in the possibility that leadership could be different.

Your leadership style became a mirror; and people saw themselves in you, and began to rise, for you didn't choose leadership because it looked glamorous. You chose it because you could no longer ignore the cracks in the foundation, the same foundation you were once told to accept, work within, and eventually protect. You chose leadership because staying silent was more dangerous than stepping up.

# PART IV: LOSS, LOVE, AND LEGACY

*Not everything survives the journey—but everything teaches you.*

# Chapter 10 – Losing My Mother

*Grief. Reflection. Identity shaken. The beginnings of healing.*

The Pain, the Mirror, and the Beginning of Healing

There are losses that fracture your timeline. There is before, and there is after; and for many of us, losing our mother is that dividing line. For all your life, she had been your north star, and it was not always easy, not always soft, but always there.

Her voice was like a metronome to your growth, her gaze a compass, and her shadow a shelter.

You didn't always understand her, you didn't always agree with her, but she was yours, and you were hers; and somewhere in that invisible tether, you knew you belonged.

When she left this world, the world itself shifted.

Not in a dramatic way. No earthquake, no explosion.

But a quiet collapse of something essential. A room that echoed differently.

You expected the grief. But you didn't expect the silence.

Not just the silence of her absence, but the silence within yourself.

The kind of silence that unsettles, that startles, and that opens old doors you had nailed shut.

Who am I now? Who am I without her?

You find yourself scanning your life backwards, as though flipping through photo albums that no longer sit on any shelf. Every moment gains new weight, even the way she stirred her coffee, the way she called your name, and the sigh she gave before offering advice.

Even the look she gave before offering correction, all of it is precious, and none of it is retrievable.

You wonder if you ever really saw her, instead of just the roles she played—mother, caregiver, disciplinarian, teacher.

You wonder if you ever really saw her, the woman behind the mask, the girl who grew into armor, and the fighter who never stopped fighting, even when the war had long ended.

Did you ever ask her what her dreams were? Did you ever ask her what she feared?

Did you ever ask her if she was okay?

She taught you survival, but she never taught you how to grieve, maybe because she never had the chance to learn it herself; or maybe because Black women don't always get to grieve; rather, they just keep going; and maybe you inherited that too.

But now, you can't just keep going, because something in you has stopped. There is a stillness you didn't choose, a stillness that asks you to pay attention; and you sit in it, reluctantly, resentfully, and then, reverently. In that stillness, her memory rises, and not like a ghost, but like a mirror.

You see her sacrifices, the exhaustion behind her strength, and the hope she held tightly, sometimes too tightly, because it was all she had. You see the fierceness that was really fear, the silence that was really shame, and the distance that was really protection. And now, you feel it, you feel all of it, the ache, the gratitude, and the confusion. You feel the guilt, the admiration, the unanswered questions, and the stories left untold. You also feel the wisdom left unspoken, the love that didn't always find words; and you begin to realize something profound:

Grief is not the enemy. It is the final form of love. It is how we carry the people we lose; and it is how we become them and remain ourselves.

You then start to hear her in your voice. You catch yourself saying things she used to say. You parent your children the way she parented you, sometimes by imitation, and sometimes by correction. You notice her in your hands, your decisions, and your laughter. You begin to understand her not just as a mother, but as a woman, and a full human being; and that changes everything. Her death doesn't end your relationship with her; rather, it transforms it.

You then begin to write. You begin to speak, not just about her death, but about her life, about the woman who worked three jobs, the woman who never took a sick day, and the woman who didn't know how to rest until she collapsed. You begin to write about the woman who prayed in the dark and smiled in the morning, and the woman who believed in you more than you believed in yourself.

You then realize that the power of a mother's love is not always in her tenderness, but sometimes it's in her tenacity, in the way she didn't let you give up, in the way she corrected you harshly because she feared the world would be harsher; and sometimes it's in the way she made you mad, and then made you whole.

You remember the way she walked into rooms, the way she sat during silence, and the way she dressed for church. You also remember the way she carried her pain with style and her joy with restraint; and how she cried when no one was watching, and laughed louder when everyone needed it most. Lastly, you remember the last time you saw her, the last words, the last touch, and the last glance; and it replays, over and over, until it settles. You then realize that your grief is not asking for an end; rather, it's asking for a home, and you begin to give it one.

You then light a candle, you tell her story, and you share her recipes. You also wear her ring, you forgive what you didn't understand, and you accept what will never be resolved.

You walk with the pain, but you no longer resist it, and in that surrender, healing begins, for healing doesn't mean forgetting; rather it means integrating, it means allowing loss to become part of your identity without letting it be the only part.

As such, you show up to life differently now, softer, more honest, and more spacious.

You no longer chase perfection, you chase meaning. You no longer fear the silence, you listen to it, and you lead differently now. You speak with more compassion. You listen with more presence; and you see pain behind other people's walls. You no longer confuse strength with hardness. You no longer confuse productivity with worth; and you now know the power of just being.

Her death broke something open, and from that opening, a deeper version of you emerged, a version that knows that legacy isn't what we build; but it is who we become, and what we pass on through our way of loving, living, forgiving, and showing up.

You didn't just lose your mother. You found the roots she left in you; and now, you water them with your tears, with your stories, with your courage, and with your care.

You live not just in memory of her, but through the memory of her. You let her be your teacher, still, and in doing so, you become the kind of ancestor she hoped to be. You begin to honor her legacy not just through words, but through your choices.

You take care of your body, even though she never had the chance to. You say "I love you" often, because she didn't always know how. You rest, because she never could. You set boundaries, because she didn't know that was allowed. You ask for help, because she never learned how. You heal, because she wasn't given the tools. And you pass it on.

You pass it on to your children, to your colleagues, to your community, and on the world, for the most powerful tribute you can give her is to live fully— In the light of her love, in the truth of her struggle, and in the clarity of your own becoming.

So yes, you lost your mother, but you also found her—in the quiet, in the sorrow, and in the parts of yourself you hadn't met until now. You found her in your leadership, in your softness, in your strength, in your tears, and in your tenderness.

You also find her in the way you now walk through this world, not afraid to feel, not afraid to love, and not afraid to remember for remembering is how you keep her close, and healing is how you carry her forward.

# Chapter 11—Breaking Down to Breath Through

*Marriage, alcohol, doubt—and how pain became a doorway*

There are times when you look in the mirror and don't recognize who's staring back. It wasn't a single moment, but a slow unraveling—the kind that sneaks up on you while life goes on. At first, it looked like fatigue, like stress, like the toll of leadership and legacy. But underneath, something deeper was stirring. Something you didn't want to face.

Marriage had become more about routine than connection. The love was real, but buried under responsibilities, expectations, and unspoken resentments. The silence between conversations, the way you passed each other in the hallway, the decisions made together but felt alone— all of it wore down the fabric of what once was sacred.

And then there was the drinking.

At first, it was just a way to relax, to take the edge off. A glass of wine here, a stiff drink after a long day. But eventually, the edge didn't soften. It sharpened. The drink became a mask—one that numbed, blurred, and let you avoid the questions that wouldn't stop whispering.

Are you happy? Who are you becoming? Is this what you imagined when you started out?

The public version of you kept functioning—promotions, recognition, praise. You smiled, delivered, led. But inside, a widening crack was forming. The wider it grew, the more exhausted you became trying to hold it all together.

Until it all broke.

Not loudly, but quietly. A night you don't talk about much; a morning of reckoning; and a truth that came not as shame, but as surrender: You couldn't live like this anymore. Something had to change.

And so began the breaking.

Therapy, honest conversations, admitting things you'd buried for years, and facing pain that wasn't just recent, but generational. It was the pressure of being the strong one, the "made it" one, the one others looked to. It was the Black man who carried not just his story, but the hopes and expectations of so many others.

It was a painful season—one where you felt exposed, where you questioned everything: your marriage, your role, your motives, your heart. You stripped away the armor; you stopped pretending you were okay; and you stopped believing that success and suffering had to coexist.

But pain—real pain—has a strange gift.

If you let it, it becomes a doorway, and not an escape, but an entry point to honesty, to clarity, and to healing.

And you walked through it.

You rebuilt, and not quickly, but intentionally. You owned your choices, you made amends, and you found ways to be whole again, and not the old version of you, but a new one—softer, stronger, and wiser. You learned to listen more than you spoke, to love with presence, not pressure, and to choose truth over performance.

You learned that breakdowns aren't failures, they're invitations, and they're wake-up calls that say: Stop performing, get honest, and return to yourself.

And slowly, you did.

The alcohol? You walked away, and not overnight, but with a commitment you honored daily. You reached out for help, you let yourself be seen, and you redefined what strength looked like—not stoicism, but vulnerability; and not control, but presence.

The marriage? It shifted. There were hard conversations. Some doors closed, others opened, and you both changed—and change, while painful, can be liberating; and you gave each other the gift of truth.

The doubt? It didn't disappear, but it no longer ran the show. You befriended it, listened to it, learned from it; and in doing so, you transformed it.

What defined you now wasn't perfection, or position, or praise. It was presence, integrity, and a fierce commitment to living from the inside out.

You started speaking more openly—at work, with friends, and on panels. You told the truth, and you let people see the whole story, not just the highlight reel. Something amazing happened: people leaned in. They saw themselves in you. They cried, they shared, and they healed too.

Your story became more than survival. It became service.

And through that service, you built trust—not just with others, but with yourself.

You no longer feared the mirror, because now, when you looked, you saw a man who had faced the fire and didn't run. You saw a man who had fallen and risen; and not despite the fall, but because of it.

The breakdown became a breakthrough.

You became a leader not because you had all the answers, but because you were willing to ask the hard questions—and live them.

You learned that we don't lead best from our strength. We lead best from our truth.

You stopped hiding.

You are someone who let pain become a doorway.

And because of that, everything has changed.

# Chapter 12 —Who I Am Now

*Father. Leader. Brother. Mentor. What still haunts you—and what still heals*

There are stories that never end, and not because they weren't finished, but because they still live in you.

This chapter isn't about arrival. It's about presence. It's about the moment you look at your life and realize that the boy who never thought he'd make it has grown into a man still learning, still healing, still becoming.

You are a father now. That title carries weight, wonder, and worry all at once. Every time your child looks at you, it feels like both a question and a promise. Will you be what they need? Can you give what you didn't receive? And the truth is, you're doing your best, and not perfectly, but with intention. You hold space for their emotions. You listen. You love, not just loudly but consistently. You are rewriting patterns without even realizing it; and some days, that alone is your victory.

You are a leader, not just by title, but by example. There are people who count on you, not because they have to, but because they've seen something in you: steadiness, empathy, and truth. You've learned that leadership isn't about power, it's about presence. It's about walking through the fire first, so others know they can survive it. It's about saying, "I don't have all the answers," and meaning it. It's about making room at the table for those who've never been invited.

You are a brother, still. Even when distance, time, and loss have rearranged the shape of your family, that identity remains. You call, you show up, and you remember birthdays. You protect, the way Loretta once protected you, and when you think of Blease, your sister who died before you truly knew her, you carry her in ways others might not understand. Her memory shaped you, her absence filled the room with questions, but also with strength. Grief doesn't end, but it evolves. It becomes part of your DNA, and somehow, it makes you more human.

You are a mentor. You didn't plan to be one, it just happened. A younger colleague asks for coffee. A student sends a message. A team member lingers after a meeting. And you hear the unspoken plea: "Can you show me how to become?" You don't have formulas, but you have lived. You have fallen and stood again, and that's what you give them—your story. You have not given the polished version, but the real one, the one with the cracks and the doubt and the decisions you're still living with.

What still haunts you? The times you didn't speak up. The love you didn't fight for. The parts of yourself you silenced because you thought they didn't fit the role you were playing. What still haunts you is the pain you dismissed because you were too busy saving others. It is the anger that still simmers when systems fail your people; and the nights when success feels like a costume and imposter syndrome tries to make a home in your heart.

But what still heals you?

Mornings where the sun touches your face and you remember to breathe.

Phone calls with old friends who remind you who you are.

Letters you write but never send.

The way your child's laugh rewrites your nervous system.

The quiet pride you feel when someone says, "Because of you, I didn't give up."

You're not finished. You're not flawless. You are in progress—and proud of it.

This is who you are now:

- A man who chose not to run from his past.
- A leader who still cries in the dark sometimes.
- A father who says, "I love you," without hesitation.
- A brother who honors memory.
- A mentor who listens more than he speaks.
- A human who understands that healing isn't a destination—it's a rhythm.

This chapter is a pause, a breath, and a hand reaching out, saying: Here I am, still here, still whole, and still healing.

And maybe, just maybe, that's more than enough.

# PART V: THE MESSAGE

*For those still climbing, still falling, still dreaming.*

## Chapter 13: Five Lessons That Carried Me

*For those still climbing, still falling, still dreaming.*

### Surviving Your Environment

You don't survive by accident. You survive by instinct, by choice, and by grace. Looking back, I realize I was never supposed to make it out—statistically speaking. However, survival wasn't just about dodging bullets or escaping bad decisions. It was also about unlearning the idea that survival was enough. I had to stop believing that making it out alive was the end goal, and start believing that healing, thriving, and giving back were also within reach.

### Dealing with Grief and Loss

Grief doesn't ask permission. It arrives uninvited, stays longer than you expect, and teaches you more than you wanted to learn. Losing my mother, losing Blease, losing the version of myself I once thought was invincible—these losses cracked me open; yet, from that crack came light, for I've learned that grief is not something you get over. It's something you carry with you, like a scar that becomes part of your story. It reminds you what matters, it humbles you, and in time, it heals you.

### Professional Setbacks

Failure is part of leadership. You didn't know that when you first started. You thought failure meant you weren't good enough. But now you understand that every setback was preparing you for the work you were truly called to do. The times you didn't get the job, the times you were misunderstood, the times you questioned your path—those were the times you were being refined. You can't lead people through fire if you've never been burned. You can't hold space for others unless you've sat in your own discomfort and made peace with it.

## Redefining Masculinity and Vulnerability

You were raised to be tough, to hold it in, and to keep moving. Yet, that definition of masculinity nearly destroyed you. It kept you silent when you needed help; and it kept you distant when you needed connection. Redefining masculinity meant embracing the parts of myself I had been told to hide—my softness, my sadness, my need for love. It meant learning that vulnerability is strength, that crying isn't weakness, and that love—especially love for yourself—is not optional.

## Moving Forward When You Feel Stuck

There were days I didn't think I could take another step. There were days when the pain was too heavy, the pressure too much, the doubt too loud. But I kept moving—sometimes out of faith, sometimes out of stubbornness, and sometimes just because someone else believed in me when I didn't. You don't have to have it all figured out to move forward. You just have to decide that staying stuck isn't an option; and then, with whatever you have left, you move. You move through the fear, through the fog, through the fatigue, and eventually, you find your way again.

These five lessons are not the end of you story. They are the threads that continue to weave your life together. They are the truths I offer to anyone still in the middle of their becoming. You are not behind. You are not broken. You are being shaped, and the shaping, though painful, is holy.

# Chapter 14: What They Never Taught Us

*The truths about power, love, race, and pain that no textbook prepared you for.*

You were taught to work hard, to follow the rules, to be respectable—and it would all pay off. But they never told you what it would feel like to be the only Black man in the room who made it. They never told you how silence would follow your voice, or how your wins would sometimes taste like survival, not victory. They never told you what it would mean to carry the weight of your community's hopes while hiding your own wounds. No, they never taught you that.

They taught you about checks and balances, about branches of government, about the Constitution—but they didn't teach you how the system feels when it fails your people. They didn't prepare you for watching young Black boys get swallowed by the same streets you barely escaped. They didn't prepare you for the grief that comes with leadership—the grief of wanting to save everyone and knowing you can't.

They never taught you what it means to rise and still feel like you're falling; or to have a title that commands respect, but still be followed in a store. They didn't teach you how to grieve the parts of yourself you lost while becoming 'successful.' They didn't teach you how to be soft in a world that only celebrates your strength. No, they didn't show you how to love yourself when you've been trained to endure, to perform, to produce.

You learned through pain, through sitting with the silence; and through watching your own people look at you like you've sold out because you made it. Yet, you still choose to love them. You still choose to show up; and you still choose to speak truth in rooms that don't know how to hold it.

What they never taught you is how deeply you would crave mentorship—and how rare it would be to find someone who saw your potential without being threatened by it. They didn't teach you how to ask for help; or that it's okay to need it; or that vulnerability isn't weakness. You had to learn that alone, and you did.

They didn't tell you that your anger would be read as aggression; that your confidence would be mistaken for arrogance; that no matter how qualified you were, someone would always question whether you belonged; and that sometimes, that someone would be you.

They didn't teach you about imposter syndrome; about internalized oppression; and about how racism can whisper through your own mind—telling you you're not good enough. You had to unlearn so much just to be able to believe in your own brilliance.

But you did learn. You learned how to breathe in the fire and not be burned. You learned how to sit at the table without losing your soul; and you learned how to lead with integrity even when no one was watching. You also learned how to be the mirror you never had, and the mentor you always needed.

You then learned that power means nothing without purpose; and that titles fade, but impact echoes. You learned that it's not about being perfect; rather, it's about being real, being honest, being present, and being willing to go back for others.

You learned that sometimes, the most radical thing you can do is rest, cry, and say, "I don't know." You learned that your humanity is not a liability, but your greatest leadership asset.

They never taught you that healing is political, that grief is sacred, and that joy is resistance. You had to live it to understand it; and now, you teach it—not with lectures, but with how you walk through the world.

So, to the young brother still doubting himself: You are not a mistake. You are not too late. You are not too broken. What they didn't teach you, you'll learn; and what you've learned, you'll pass on.

Because that's the real curriculum; the one written in scars and hope; in prayers and protest; in your grandmother's hands; in your mother's tears; an in the laughter that survived even the hardest days.

You are the textbook now, the teacher, the truth-teller, and your story is a masterclass in becoming whole. Even when the world tried to break you in pieces, you rose anyway, and you will keep rising, because though they never taught you—now you know.

# PART VI: THE BECOMING

*Becoming doesn't always look like winning—but it always looks like truth.*

# Chapter 15: The Weight and Wonder of Becoming

*How far you've come—and the parts of you still catching up.*

Becoming is never a straight line.

You thought becoming would feel like certainty, like walking into a room and knowing you deserve to be there; or like wearing your name on your chest and feeling proud, not performative; but it wasn't like that—not entirely. It was complicated, it was messy, and it was sacred.

You thought it would be about accomplishment—crossing off dreams like items on a grocery list—Degree, career, marriage, house, and title. You thought those things would make you feel like you'd arrived; but the truth is, every milestone came with its own unraveling. Every promotion made you question if you belonged; and every praise brought up the ghost of someone who said you'd never be enough.

There's a strange weight in arriving where you once only dreamed to stand. There's wonder in it, too—wonder that you made it at all, wonder at the child in you who still flinches, and wonder at how you keep showing up, even when you doubt. There is no applause in the quiet moments, no gold stars for trying again, and again, and again; but still, you persist.

You now understand that becoming isn't a finish line. It's a rhythm, a return, and a remembrance. It is a remembrance of who you are underneath the armor, of who you promised yourself you'd be, and of the person others hoped you'd forget. Becoming is less about arrival, and more about reunion—with your truth, your softness, and your purpose.

It is a remembering of who you were before the world told you who you had to be. It is a remembering of the boy with big eyes and bigger questions; and it is a remembering of the quiet ache that told you there must be more. It is also a remembering of your capacity for joy, for presence, and for love that doesn't apologize for being loud.

You carry many selves within you.—the achiever, the provider, the protector, the survivor, the dreamer, and the doubter. You carry within you the boy who wanted to run and the man who stood his ground; and all of them show up, sometimes all at once; and you've learned to listen to them, not to silence them; and you've made peace with your contradictions.

Though some parts of you still hide, still ache, still wait for safety—you're learning to lead from those places too. That's the wonder—that the most powerful version of you isn't the one who's perfected; rather, it's the one who's present, the one who says, "This hurts," and still chooses to love. It is the one who says, "I'm scared," and still shows up. It is also the one who chooses softness even when the world rewards stone.

You became someone who no longer needs to pretend; someone who says no when it costs your peace; and someone who lets others shine, because you know their light doesn't dim yours. You also became someone who understands that vulnerability is not weakness, but it's revolution.

You carry the weight of your ancestors, their hope, their trauma, their brilliance, and their burdens. You are their wildest dream and their unfinished business; and sometimes, that's heavy; while other times, it's holy. You are then the product of survival and the evidence of possibility; and you are learning to make space for both.

You are becoming, not in spite of those contradictions, but because of them; not in spite of your wounds, but through them; and not in spite of your fear, but by befriending it.

Moreover, there are moments that don't make the resume, but they changed everything. There is the night you almost gave up, the conversation that cracked something open; and the forgiveness you gave when it wasn't asked for. There are also the quiet mornings when you sat with yourself and didn't run.

As such, you still carry the weight of questions you never asked. You still carry the ache of doors that closed before you were ready; and you still carry the guilt of opportunities you almost missed because you didn't believe you deserved them. Further, you carry the pressure to be excellent, to be the first, to be the proof; and sometimes that pressure feels like love; while other times it feels like a cage.

And still—you marvel. You marvel at your own becoming; at how you laugh again; and at how you protect your peace like it's sacred—because it is. You marvel at how you hold space for others without losing yourself; at how you speak the truth even when your voice trembles; and at how you say, 'This is who I am now,' with no apology.

The way you lead has changed. You don't need to be the loudest voice in the room, for you understand that wisdom is not about knowing everything, it's about staying curious. You lift others as you climb, you mentor without needing to be praised, you create space for the quiet ones, and you know the power of being underestimated.

You once thought healing would feel like 'done;' like something you achieved. Now you know healing is a rhythm, a ritual, a return. Some days you rise radiant, some days you're still reaching, but you are showing up, you are staying open, and you are becoming.

At some point, you stopped asking 'What should I do?' and started asking 'Who am I becoming?' That shift changed everything. It made room for your soul. It made room for joy; and it made room for truth.

There are still parts of you that flinch at kindness. There are still parts that brace for rejection; and there are still parts that worry it might all fall apart; but those parts are no longer in control, they're just passengers now, instead of drivers.

Your legacy isn't a monument, it's a mirror; it's the people who felt seen because of you; it's the systems that shifted because you stayed; and it's the lives that softened because you said, 'Me too.'

You are not just a man who made it. You are a man who *is making it*, in real time, with cracked hands and soft eyes, with tired feet and a beating heart, and with stories you're still writing and lessons you're still learning.

This is the weight and wonder of becoming: it doesn't end, it evolves, and it includes you, all of you.

So keep becoming. Keep breaking. Keep building. Keep breathing.

Because even now, even here, especially here—you are enough.

# Chapter 16: Finding Home Within

*Redefining what safety, self-love, and peace really mean.*

There comes a time when the climb outward turns inward; when the question is no longer, "What more can I achieve?" but instead, "Where do I feel at peace?" This chapter is about that moment.

For much of my life, I was building; building resilience; building credibility; and building something bigger than myself; but I hadn't asked what all the building was for. I hadn't asked what it meant to feel at home—in my own body, my own mind, my own spirit.

This chapter is about the search for that kind of home, the kind you carry with you.

Home is not just a place; it's a knowing; and it's a relationship with yourself that says: no matter what, you belong.

The world told you early on that belonging was conditional, conditional on performance, on obedience, on being tough, and on hiding my tenderness. I bought into that for too long. I wore the masks I was taught to wear: The Strong Black Man, the Overachiever, the Public Servant, the Mentor, and the Rock.

However, what happens when the rock starts to crack? What happens when the roles no longer fit? What happens when you wake up and wonder who you are beneath it all?

That's where the work began.

You started asking better questions. Not "How do I fix myself?" but "What parts of me have never been welcomed?" Not "What should I be doing?" but "What does my soul want to say?"

I had to grieve the time I spent living for others. I had to make room for the parts of me that didn't fit the public image, the scared parts, the curious parts, the parts that still missed my mother, and the parts that longed to be held.

And slowly, something softened, and something began to settle.

You then stopped chasing peace outside of you and started creating it within you.

You started making rituals out of presence—walking slowly, breathing deeply, and cooking intentionally. You began to speak to yourself as you would a child you loved. You let go of needing to prove anything; and in the quiet moments, you began to feel it: Home.

I don't share this as someone who's figured it all out. I still have days when the old beliefs come roaring back, when the critic gets loud, and when the fear creeps in. Yet, now I know what to do. I come back to myself. I remember: I am already enough.

There's power in coming home to yourself. It's the kind of power no one can give you and no one can take away.

So if you're reading this and you're still searching, I want to say this clearly: You're not lost. You're in process. You are not broken. You are becoming. And the home you're looking for is already inside you.

Sit with yourself. Ask the real questions. Let yourself be seen.

You may just find you've been home all along.

# Chapter 17: The Courage to Tell the Truth

*Living without shame. Speaking with heart. Owning your full story.*

You spend so much of your life hiding, and not always on purpose, but sometimes, hiding looks like performing; while other times, it looks like rising through the ranks, meeting expectations, smiling on cue; and sometimes, still, it looks like success.

But inside, there's a truth you haven't spoken; a version of your story you keep tucked away, and not because you're ashamed, but because you're afraid it might change how the world sees you. Or maybe how you see yourself.

The courage to tell the truth isn't about standing in front of a crowd, it's about facing the mirror.

It's about saying: This is what I've been through, this is what hurt, this is what I learned, and this is what I still carry.

It's about reclaiming the parts of your story that didn't get airtime in the highlight reel. It's about breaking the silence that shaped your inner world more than anyone knows.

For years, you told the story that was palatable, the one that made others comfortable, and the version that fit the mold; but your real story—the one with the failures, the fears, the tears, the doubts—is the one that can actually set people free; and perhaps, most importantly, it's the one that sets *you* free.

Because when you tell the truth, you stop apologizing for existing, you stop minimizing your brilliance to make others feel safe, and you stop performing strength and finally begin *being* strong.

Telling the truth doesn't mean dumping your trauma or seeking pity. It means offering your story as a lighthouse, not a spotlight. You're not trying to be seen; you're trying to help others see.

And the only way to do that—is to be honest.

You remember the first time you told someone about the lowest point in your life. You remember the fear that gripped you, the shame that almost swallowed you, but also, the look in their eyes—their tears, their nods, and their own confession that they'd been there too.

That moment taught you: Truth is the bridge, and it is not power, not perfection, not position, but Truth.

Truth builds trust. It softens hearts, it dissolves shame, it creates connection, and it restores hope.

You once thought leadership meant always having the answer. But now you know: leadership is being brave enough to tell the truth even when it's messy. You've learned that you can lead with your scars, not in spite of them; and you've learned that you don't need to hide anymore. The version of you that survived, healed, grew, and keeps going is worthy of being known. Fully, fiercely, and freely.

So, tell your truth.

Tell it for the ones who can't yet find the words.

Tell it for the child inside you who waited too long to be heard.

Tell it for the future you who deserves to live unburdened.

Tell it because someone out there is drowning, and your truth might be the lifeline.

Tell it because *you* are worth being known; and that's what this whole book has been about; and it is not just the story of one man, but the story of all of us, the story we hide, the story we fear, and the story we hope might mean something.

And it does.

Because truth is not just a revelation.

It's a revolution.

# Chapter 18: Rising, Again

*Permission to start over, to rest, to rejoice, and to reclaim joy.*

Life doesn't hand out neat resolutions. It hands you wake-up calls, warnings, wounds, and reminders; and sometimes, it hands you the chance to rise again.

You thought you had already overcome so much— childhood trauma, academic failure, imposter syndrome, and the invisible tax of being a Black man in leadership. You had lost a mother, endured grief, and made peace with your past, but life was not done with you yet.

There's a kind of fatigue that doesn't come from work but from soul-tiredness. There is that moment when you're driving to another meeting, another event, another responsibility, and something inside whispers: *"What about you?"*

You begin to feel the ache of self-abandonment, the cost of being strong for everyone else, and the places in you still needing rest, tending, and truth.

This chapter is not about a dramatic event. It's not about a rock bottom or a crash.

It's about the slow realization that you had stopped living for yourself. You were fulfilling roles, checking boxes, upholding expectations— but forgetting joy.

You began to choose what to say yes to, you began to cancel, you sat in silence, you wrote again, and you walked alone without your phone. You rediscovered Sabbath, not religiously, but relationally, and you let the stillness hold you; and in that stillness, you began to rise, not as a leader or a father or a brother or a commissioner, but as a man, a man who weeps in gratitude, a man who no longer hides from fear, and a man who gives himself permission to feel lightness, and even laughter.

You redefined ambition, not as accomplishment, but as alignment. You stopped seeking applause and started seeking awe. You forgave people who never said sorry; and you forgave parts of yourself you didn't even know were hurting. You chose to rise, not as the world sees rising, but as your soul defines it.

Today, rising looks like sitting still, choosing your yes, laughing loudly, protecting your mornings, and reconnecting with old friends. It means letting yourself fall in love with life, with people, and with possibility.

It's not always easy. Some days, the shadow calls louder than the light. Some days, doubt still drapes its arms over your shoulders; but now you know what to do. You breathe, you write, you walk, and you call.

You remember, and you rise again, and again, and again.

You are not behind.

You are not too late.

You are not broken.

You are becoming.

And that is enough reason to rise again.

# Chapter 19: The Next Mountain

*Some journeys don't end—they transform.*

Just when you think you've arrived, another summit reveals itself, a new calling, a deeper purpose, and a fresh horizon. This is the mountain I stand before now.

I used to believe the climb was about proving something, to my past, to my pain, and to those who doubted. Yet, the older I get, the more I understand: It was never about proving, it was about becoming. Now, the next mountain isn't external, it isn't another title, another achievement, or another position. It's internal.

The next mountain is humility, compassion, and presence. It is about making space for others to rise. It's listening more than speaking, serving without needing to be seen, and trusting that the seeds you've sown will bloom in others, long after you're gone.

It's knowing that legacy isn't a building named after you; rather, it's the lives you've touched.

Here's what I've also learned: the higher you go, the softer your steps must become, for the view is clearer, but the air is thinner. You have to breathe more deeply, walk more slowly, and love more fully.

You don't climb the next mountain to conquer it, you climb it to honor it.

So I stand here now, not to be celebrated, but to remind you:

There is always more, more to learn, more to heal, and more to give.

And maybe that's the point. The next mountain humbles you, strips away illusion, and calls forth your most authentic self; the self who no longer needs applause; the self who finds joy in the quiet; and the self who builds without needing credit.

This is my next mountain, not for glory, but for grace; and not for validation, but for love; and if you're reading this, maybe you've reached your next mountain, too.

I'm walking beside you.

Let's climb.

# Chapter 20: You Were Always the Light
*Closing Reflections*

You've made it to the final chapter, but let's be clear, this is not an ending. If anything, it's a continuation, a reminder, and a torch being passed to you, for the truth is, you were always the light.

From the beginning, even when the shadows of life tried to convince you otherwise—through the trauma, the grief, the missteps, the doubt—you carried something unbreakable inside you. Maybe, just maybe, no one told you often enough; or you were too busy surviving to believe it; but I see it, and if you're still here, reading these words, then some part of you sees it too.

This book wasn't just about my story. It was about possibility. Yours. Mine. Ours.

You were always the light even when you were lost, it was there. Even when you hurt someone you loved, it was there. Even when you broke down, gave up, fell behind, it remained.

What I want for you is what I came to want for myself:

- That you honor your scars without letting them define you.
- That you feel your grief but don't get trapped inside it.
- That you remember healing is messy and nonlinear, and so is growth.
- That you speak your truth, even if your voice shakes.
- That you lead with purpose, even if no one follows at first.

### The Promise of Purpose

Purpose is not a title. It's not a salary. It's not what people call you when you walk into a room. Purpose is what you bring with you. It's how you show up. It's the lives you touch when no one's watching.

It's the decision you make, day after day, to live with integrity and love. Even when it's hard.

Maybe you're in a dark place right now. Maybe you feel like it's too late, too broken, too much, but let me say this as clearly as I can:

The light is still in you.

It's waiting to be remembered.

So take a breath.

Stand up.

Keep going.

Because the world needs what only you can give. And you were always the light.

Thank you for reading.

Thank you for surviving.

Thank you for becoming.

You are not alone. You never were.

And I love you from the bottom of my heart.

Gary

# Conclusion

*Never Give Up*

There is a rhythm to life that only reveals itself when we stop running and start listening. Through every closed door, every lost moment, and every quiet storm, I have learned this: you are never done until you decide you're done. And even then—life may still have one more chapter to write through you.

This book is not just a memoir. It is a mirror. It reflects the faces, names, and communities that made me. It tells the story of a boy from Brooklyn who dared to believe that compassion could be a form of strength—and that leadership rooted in love is the most radical kind there is.

I didn't always know the way. I still don't. But I've come to understand that the greatest leaders are not those who rise above others, but those who walk beside them—who hold the line when the weight is heavy, and who remind the world that no one gets left behind.

We all have a story to tell. Some stories begin in silence. Some start with pain. Some are carried for generations, waiting for one voice brave enough to break the pattern.

This is my voice. This is my story. But it is also yours.

If there is one message I pray this book leaves with you, it is this:

No matter who you are.

No matter where you start.

No matter what they said about you or what you've said to yourself—

You can still become the change.

You can still lead with dignity.

You can still rise.

You can still love.

And you must—Never. Give. Up.

# Epilogue: The Road Ahead

If you've made it this far, thank you—for listening, for holding space, and for walking alongside me through these pages. This has not only been a telling of my story. It has been an unburdening, a remembering, and a recommitment to the very values that continue to shape my life: resilience, faith, service, and love.

What lies ahead is not simply about titles or accomplishments. It's about how we show up—in our communities, in our families, and within ourselves. It's about refusing to become bitter when the world is unfair. It's about choosing dignity when others expect defeat. It's about becoming the kind of person who doesn't just survive the storm, but builds shelter for others while it rages.

I don't pretend to have all the answers. I'm still becoming. Still healing. Still learning. But I do know this: Every setback contains the seed of a higher purpose. Every wound, when faced with honesty and grace, can become a doorway to deeper compassion. And every one of us has the power to lead—not just with our resumes, but with our hearts.

Once again, my hope is that Never Give Up is more than a memoir. I hope it's a mirror for anyone who's ever questioned whether they mattered. I hope it's a manual for every young person who thinks leadership is out of reach. I hope it's a reminder to every adult that your past doesn't disqualify you—sometimes it qualifies you in ways no classroom ever could.

The road ahead will still test us. We will still be underestimated, misunderstood, and occasionally misrepresented. But we will move forward anyway. We will rise anyway. We will serve anyway. We will lead anyway. Because the world does not need more perfect people. It needs real people—rooted, resilient, and ready to become the change.

To every reader: I see you. Keep going. You were never alone. And no matter what—never give up.

With love and respect,

Gary

# Invitation to the Reader

You've now walked beside me—through heartbreak and healing, through poverty and purpose, through setbacks and soaring. Thank you for holding space for this story.

But this isn't just my story.

It's yours, too.

It belongs to anyone who has ever felt invisible, underestimated, or unsure. It belongs to anyone who has faced the mirror and wondered, Can I really make it? It belongs to anyone who still carries scars but dares to keep showing up anyway.

You are the reason this book exists.

And my greatest hope is that it reminded you: Never Give Up.

## Reflection

Before you turn this page—or close this book—take a breath.

Ask yourself:

- What moment in this book moved something in me?
- What parts of my own journey have I been hiding—or denying—out of fear or shame?
- Where have I already risen, and not yet honored my own strength?
- Who can I lift, now that I know I can rise?

This book is not a conclusion. It's a beginning. Let it be a spark.

## Call to Action

We need you.

We need leaders who carry both courage and compassion. We need people who will hold space for pain and possibility. We need stories like yours—unpolished, powerful, and real.

So I ask you:

1. Tell your truth.
2. Stand in your purpose.
3. Be the change—even if your voice shakes, even if no one claps at first.

Because someone, somewhere, is waiting for your light.

## Review Request

If this book meant something to you—if it helped you feel seen, or gave you hope, or inspired you to keep going—I would be honored if you would share that.

Please take 60 seconds to leave a review on Amazon or wherever you purchased this book.

Your words matter. They help others find their way to this story when they need it most.

And if you know someone who is struggling, growing, or leading in silence—pass this book on.

Together, let's make sure no one ever forgets:

Never Give Up.

—

With gratitude and purpose,

Gary Jenkins

# Final Acknowledgments

To my BFF, Kimberly Hardy Regester Wiltshire—
There are friendships, and then there are lifelines.
You have been mine.

Thank you for never leaving my side when things got rough—
even when I didn't always show up as the "best" BFF.
Your unwavering presence, patience, and belief in me
have carried me through more than words can say.

You reminded me that true friendship is not about perfection—
but about grace, endurance, and showing up over and over again.
I am better because of you.

You are a gift.

With deepest love and gratitude,

Gary

# Reader Integration Toolkit

**Bridging the Message to Your Life**

### 1. Guided Reflection Prompts

Use these questions to deepen your personal connection to the themes in *Never Give Up*:

- What in my story felt most personal to you—and why?
- When was the last time you almost gave up—but didn't?
- What's a past challenge you survived that you don't give yourself enough credit for?
- Who are your "Garys"—people who lifted you when you were low?
- Where in your life right now are you being called to rise?

✐ Write your responses in a journal, or share them in a community dialogue group.

### 2. Personal Action Plan

Create your personal "Never Give Up" roadmap with the following template:

| Step | Area of Life | Challenge | Small Step I Can Take This Week | Support Needed |
|------|-------------|-----------|--------------------------------|----------------|
|      |             |           |                                |                |
|      |             |           |                                |                |
|      |             |           |                                |                |

➡ Copy and complete this table in your journal or planner.

### 3. Resilience Anchors

Identify your current "anchors"—people, practices, or mindsets that keep you grounded.

- ♂ People who remind me I am not alone:
- 🖐 Practices that help me reset:
- 🧠 Mindsets I want to cultivate:

### 4. Weekly Courage Check-In

Each week, ask yourself:
- What did I face with courage?
- Where did I struggle—but keep going?
- What am I proud of, no matter how small?
- What do I need to remind myself of right now?

✅ Use this for weekly journaling or in team meetings, peer groups, or family check-ins.

### 5. Community Impact Reflection

Take Gary's story into the world by asking:
- Who in my community needs to know they are not alone?
- How can I show up for them this week?
- What systems do I belong to that need more empathy, equity, or healing?
- What legacy do I want to leave behind?

💡 Even one small act of connection can transform someone's path.

### 6. Your Never Give Up Commitment

Write your own commitment statement:
- "I commit to…"
- "I will remember that…"
- "When I feel like giving up, I will…"

Sign it. Tape it to your mirror. Share it with a trusted friend.

# Appendix: Tools, Exercises, Charts, and Frameworks

## Tools

1. The Resilience Wheel: Identify your sources of strength across six domains—Faith, Family, Friends, Focus, Fitness, and Forgiveness.
2. The Mirror Test: Ask yourself, "Am I living in alignment with the person I truly want to be?"
3. Purpose Pulse Check: A quick 3-question daily check-in:
   - Did I act with purpose today?
   - Did I serve someone else today?
   - Did I move forward, even in a small way?

## Exercises

### 1. Guided Journaling Prompts:

- What's one moment I almost gave up—and what kept me going?
- Who in my life embodies resilience? What have they taught me?
- What does 'never give up' mean to me now vs. five years ago?

### 2. Courage Letter:

Write a letter to your past self from your present perspective. Highlight how far you've come.

### 3. The 3Rs Reflection:

- Recognize: Acknowledge a painful or difficult memory.
- Reframe: Shift the meaning of that memory into a source of learning.
- Rise: Identify one action you can take that honors your growth.

# Charts

## 1. Weekly Resilience Tracker:

| Day | Challenge Faced | Response Chosen | Lesson Learned |
|---|---|---|---|
| Monday | | | |
| Tuesday | | | |
| Wednesday | | | |
| Thursday | | | |
| Friday | | | |
| Saturday | | | |
| Sunday | | | |

## 2. Self-Check: Resilience Scorecard

| Dimension | Low (1) | Medium (2) | High (3) |
|---|---|---|---|
| Emotional Control | | | |
| Mental Toughness | | | |
| Faith in Purpose | | | |
| Support Network | | | |

**Frameworks**

**1. The 5P Model of Resilient Leadership:**

- Purpose: Clarity in why you do what you do.
- People: Surrounding yourself with support and mentors.
- Perspective: Reframing obstacles as growth opportunities.
- Practices: Daily routines that anchor your mental wellness.
- Persistence: The discipline to stay the course.

**2. The SWEET Layers of Transformation:**

- Conscious: Behavior-level tools and checklists.
- Preconscious: Beliefs, habits, and conditioning.
- Unconscious: Healing inner wounds and hidden patterns.
- Existential: Meaning, contribution, and identity.

# Recommended Reading

- Dreams from My Father by Barack Obama
- The Purpose Driven Life by Rick Warren
- Man's Search for Meaning by Viktor Frankl
- The Gifts of Imperfection by Brené Brown
- Just Mercy by Bryan Stevenson
- Between the World and Me by Ta-Nehisi Coates
- Start with Why by Simon Sinek
- The Four Agreements by Don Miguel Ruiz
- The Seven Habits of Highly Effective People by Stephen R. Covey
- The Power of Now by Eckhart Tolle
- The Autobiography of Malcolm X as told to Alex Haley
- Strength to Love by Martin Luther King, Jr.
- I Know Why the Caged Bird Sings by Maya Angelou
- Lead from the Outside by Stacey Abrams
- Caste by Isabel Wilkerson
- The Fire Next Time by James Baldwin
- Unbound by Tarana Burke
- A Promised Land by Barack Obama

# About the Author

Gary P. Jenkins is currently the Chief Administrative Officer at Urban Pathways, a local nonprofit organization in New York City that provides critical services to New Yorkers in need of social service programs which includes housing and mental health services.

Prior to joining Urban Pathways, Gary was appointed by Mayor Eric Adams in January of 2022 as Commissioner of the New York City Department of Social Services (DSS), which oversees both the Human Resources Administration (HRA) and Department of Homeless Services (DHS). In this capacity, he was responsible for leading the largest local social services agency in the country. HRA serves over 3 million New Yorkers through the administration of major public assistance programs and strives to combat poverty and income inequality in New York City. DHS is the largest municipal shelter system in the nation and works to prevent homelessness, when possible, address street homelessness, provide safe temporary shelter, and connect New Yorkers experiencing homelessness to suitable housing. Together, DSS-HRA-DHS have a combined staff headcount of nearly 15,000 and a combined operating budget of nearly $13 billion.

Gary's 30-plus-year history with DSS-HRA-DHS began with a front-line position in HRA, where he rose through the ranks to become Administrator of HRA, eventually reaching the organization's pinnacle when he was appointed to serve as Commissioner of DSS. During his tenure as Commissioner, he led the agency's response to multiple crises, including the COVID-19 public health emergency and a humanitarian crisis when thousands of asylum seekers entered the DHS shelter system.

Gary is also a proud member of Phi Beta Sigma Fraternity Inc for well over 38 years and currently serves as the Vice President of his local chapter, Kappa Beta Sigma (The Brooklyn Sigmas) located in Brooklyn, NY.

Gary received his master's in public administration from Metropolitan College of New York in 2006 and his bachelor's degree from John Jay College of Criminal Justice in 1999. In 2022, he was granted a Doctor in Humane Letters from Metropolitan College of New York.

He resides in Brooklyn, New York, with his wife and three adult daughters.

www.ingramcontent.com/pod-product-compliance
Lightning Source LLC
Chambersburg PA
CBHW030316130626
46549CB00002B/892